LIFESKILLS

?2

HUMAN HORIZONS SERIES

LIFESKILLS

A Positive Approach

MONICA MACNAMARA
Drawings by Moira Macnamara

A Condor Book
Souvenir Press (E&A) Ltd

I dedicate this book with gratitude to my parents
Peter and Angela
whose consistent interest, encouragement and support
have given me the confidence in life to take on new and
challenging tasks.

First published 1995 by Souvenir Press
(Educational & Academic) Ltd,
43 Great Russell Street, London WC1B 3PA
and simultaneously in Canada

ISBN 0 285 63213 2

Photoset by Rowland Phototypesetting Ltd,
Bury St Edmunds, Suffolk

Printed in Great Britain by
The Guernsey Press Co. Ltd, Guernsey, Channel Islands

Contents

Acknowledgements

While writing this book, I received encouragement, support and practical help from a range of sources and I would like to take this opportunity to sincerely thank the people and organisations concerned.

- St Michael's House, the organisation for which I work, who facilitated the writing of this book by providing me with a range of valuable resources. I particularly thank Pat O'Loughlin for his part in securing for me a period of secondment to the Research Department which enabled me to get the project well under way.
- The trainees of Templeogue House, the branch of St Michael's House in which I work, whose trust and openness over the years have given me great insight into the lives of adults who have learning disabilities.
- The manager and staff of Templeogue House who have generously shared their information and experience. They have consistently shown interest in this and other aspects of my work and given me valuable feedback on numerous aspects of Lifeskills training.
- The Research Department of St Michael's House where I was based when writing the book. Patricia Noonan-Walsh and Sue Jones provided hospitality, facilities, information and unfailing encouragement throughout the process.
- The stalwart critical readers, Gen O'Meara and Susie Kelly who spent hours, long into the night and early morning, scrutinising the script. They gave of their time so generously, contributing both expertise in this field of work and an excellent standard of written English to ensure an end product which reads well and is easily understood.
- Other colleagues and friends, Letitia Swift, Elizabeth

O'Loughlin and Cariona Neary who read sections of the book and provided me with additional information and valuable feedback.

- The illustrator, Moira Macnamara, who quickly achieved a very good understanding of the points that I was attempting to convey, and took time to illustrate these points so well. Moira's illustrations give the script a great vitality, they made me smile and I hope they will have the same effect on you.

- My husband, Gerry, who consistently assured me that I was capable of the task. My writing gave Gerry a valuable opportunity to improve his home and child-minding skills! Without his facilitation and support the task would not have been manageable.

- And several others—Agnes Noone, Eileen O'Callaghan, Sheelagh Kelly, Nuala Cardiff and other family, friends and colleagues too numerous to mention by name—who showed interest and supported me in various ways in the writing of this book.

Many thanks to you all.

Preface

This handbook is intended for parents, teachers and helpers of adults who have learning disabilities. It outlines an approach to Lifeskills training which strives to achieve greater independence and a better quality of life for the focus person.

The content of the book is, to a large extent, based on common sense. It has evolved from years of 'hands on' experience, working with adults who have learning disabilities, to whom a great deal of my knowledge can be directly attributed. They have helped me to discover how to bring learning alive for them and to appreciate the magic which even small achievements give to their lives.

The book aims in a practical and user-friendly way to:

- Identify Lifeskills.
- Examine and simplify the vast network of Lifeskills.
- Discuss a trainee-centred approach to Lifeskills training.
- Provide a structured framework for getting to know the trainee better.
- Examine each stage in the development of a Lifeskills training programme.
- Give a range of examples of the practical application of this type of programme.
- Identify problems which might arise and suggest possible solutions.
- Encourage and support parents, teachers and helpers in the training of Lifeskills.
- Provide information on materials and resources available.

Lifeskills training has been at the centre of my work for over ten years. The adults with learning disabilities, with whom I work, vary in age, background and capability. Like most people working in this field, I have encountered such problems as apathy, slow progress, lack of motivation, poor resources, frustration and resistance to change. To be of use, this book must be practical and positive, outlining systems which genuinely meet the needs of the individual and are possible to put into operation. It is of little value to describe in detail an elaborate approach which sounds marvellous, theoretically, but cannot be implemented in the real world!

I hope that the book will empower the reader to feel that he or she *can* bring about change and enhance the quality of the lives of people who have learning disabilities. I hope it demonstrates the positive impact of this change in their lives. The approach to training which it outlines is built on a firm foundation of total respect for and acceptance of all people, the principles of which are detailed in the introduction and which I hope will be in evidence throughout the book.

In the interest of clarity, I refer to the person with a learning disability as the 'trainee' and to the person who is offering training, whether it be parent, supervisor, teacher, helper or other, as the 'instructor'. For the same reason I refer to the trainee as male and the instructor as female, except where 'Real Life Examples' demand otherwise. These 'real life examples' are drawn directly from my own experience. The names used are fictitious.

Although the book refers specifically to adults who have learning disabilities, its approach could also apply to a range of others who need to achieve greater independence—children with learning disabilities, people with brain damage or mental illness, or those being reintroduced to community life following long-term institutionalisation. The principles of normalisation and integration which run through the book are the ideals towards which today's modern health and education services are aspiring.

Introduction

There has been a tendency over many years for responsible bodies to provide services on a large-scale basis for devalued groups. These include people with disabilities, law-breakers, people who are mentally ill, travellers and others. The motivation is generally the good of society or ease of management of the problem.

In reviewing the history of large-scale provision of services, it is common to find negative institutional practices such as block treatment of service users, rigid daily routines, excessive social distance between staff and service users, limited opportunities for choice and a range of other de-personalising practices. Even today, large-scale service provision often focuses on *caring* rather than *enabling*. Although better disguised, a lot of emphasis is still placed on ease of management and organisational routine. Have you ever experienced any of the following de-personalising practices?

- Grouping people together by some convenient label.
- Making decisions for people without reference to them.
- The needs of the organisation being put before the needs of the individual.
- Most time and attention being given to the individual whose behaviour makes group management more difficult.
- Concentrating on what is 'wrong' with an individual, rather than on his or her strengths and potential.

Real Life Example

Owen is 28 years old, living at home with his parents. He hopes that some day he will be able to live on his own or with a group of friends. He has discussed this with his parents who know that it is a realistic option, as they will not be around for ever, but do not like to think about it.

Owen's mother knows that he has a lot to learn in the running of the house and yet she finds it very difficult to give him the opportunity to learn. She claims:

'He makes such a mess if he is cooking.'

'His bed looks such a heap when he makes it himself.'

'He puts all the wrong colours together if he chooses his own clothes.'

'If he does the vacuuming, I have to go over it again myself.'

And so she continues to run the house herself.

This is a clear but very common example of management issues being put before an individual's needs. It can happen in various ways at home, at work or in the community. In this case, the efficient management of Owen's home is given priority over Owen's need to learn.

A vicious circle is created whereby:

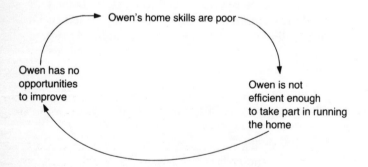

Owen's home skills are poor

Owen has no opportunities to improve

Owen is not efficient enough to take part in running the home

In a home, service or community which is management-orientated, you can change to a trainee-centred approach by acknowledging the trainee's personal identity and providing assistance in developing this. Such an ideal lies behind this book which also strives to empower individuals to establish a sense of direction and an ability to speak up and make choices. It outlines in clear steps how to put this approach into practice. As I said in the Preface, total respect for and acceptance of all people must remain at the core.

1 The importance of personal identity

Each of us strives to have a personal identity, a valued role among a network of people. The way a person sees himself is largely determined by the way he is seen by others. As G. J. Mouly comments in his book *Psychology for Effective Teaching*, 'The level of expectation which the individual sets for himself determines his relative success not only in the performance of a given task, but also as a person, this in turn determines the kind of self-concept he is likely to develop.' If an individual is facilitated in developing his personal identity, a reinforcing cycle results:

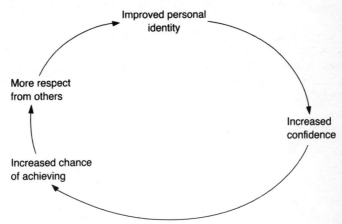

If, on the other hand, he is constantly being told that he is slow, different or a failure, it is likely that he will see himself in that way.

People with a learning disability often have an undeservedly bad reputation and are seen and treated as second-class citizens. The instructor must strive to change this by encouraging the trainee to improve his personal identity, a process in which Lifeskills training plays an important part by restoring dignity and enabling the trainee to enjoy the same status as other valued members of the family, the workplace or the community.

A key aspect of one's personal identity is the opportunity and ability to make choices with regard to big and small issues in one's own life. A successful Lifeskills training programme is built around the trainee making choices.

2   The importance of one's own community

The community should be seen as a vast resource which is equally available to all its members and which each individual must make his or her own. If a person cannot participate in his community, the problem lies not with him but rather with the type and extent of the support structured around him. Lifeskills training explores the community with the individual, identifying the supports needed to enhance his quality of life. It then works to put these supports in place.

Integration and inclusion
Integration is 'restoring to wholeness'. In terms of Lifeskills training, it is the process by which people are gradually re-introduced to the community and familiarised with community practices.

Judith Snow, an inclusion consultant in Canada, in her work *Structuring an Inclusive World*, differentiates between integration and inclusion: 'Integration describes the activities which are undertaken in order to support people being included. The concept of inclusion goes beyond integration, it is the end state to which we aspire.' She goes on to say, 'Everyone is a participant in this world, everyone belongs and everyone contributes.'

The process of integration is sometimes seen as a favour, or a special effort being made for people who have learning disabilities and other isolated groups. In fact, the absence of people with disabilities from the community renders that community incomplete. The opportunities for other community members to care and facilitate are diminished, so that they become less tolerant of flaws and more inclined to take well-being for granted. Therefore, integration and subsequent inclusion should be recognised as beneficial for everyone. When services or families isolate people with disabilities from their communities, all parties lose out.

3   The importance of a positive outlook

Far too often, the person with a learning disability is identified only by his problems. The resulting help or training is usually deficit-driven, concentrating on what is wrong and how it can be 'fixed'. Lifeskills training focuses on *capacity searching*—that is, looking beyond what a person can do and identifying his or her potential to achieve more.

Self-empowerment
Caring for people implies doing things for them, whereas empowering, which this book advocates, is enabling people to do things for themselves. It is the process by which a person gradually takes greater control of his or her own life.

It involves:

a Evaluating one's present situation.
b Identifying alternatives.
c Choosing one option.
d Working on that choice.

Self-empowerment is a process, not an end state. One does not become 'self-empowered', but behaves in a more empowered way. The more empowered a person is, the more fulfilling his or her life will become. In choosing to train in a way which empowers the trainee, the instructor has already made a significant step forward.

Facing the Challenge, edited by Roger Blunden and David Allen, summarises three similar values which it upholds in developing an effective individualised service for people who have a learning disability:

1 People with learning disabilities have the same human value as anyone else.
2 People with learning disabilities have a right and a need to live with others in the community.
3 Services must recognise the individuality of people with learning disabilities and strive to develop this.

Before embarking on the practical steps of this book, you need to examine your own basic values concerning people with learning disabilities and how these will affect the way in which you approach Lifeskills training. You may not have the time or energy to change the world, but if you ensure that your *own* approach is a positive one, based on genuine respect, then you *will* be able to bring about change for the better in the life of one or more individuals.

1   The Lifeskills Network

In my experience of working with adults who have learning disabilities, I have encountered quite a range of terms used to describe the skills required by an individual to live as full and independent a life as possible—social skills, coping skills, independent living skills, daily living skills, survival skills and many more.

There is no right or wrong way to define all or part of this vast network of skills, but for the purpose of this book and in the interest of a confident approach to skills training, it is essential to select a clear, all-inclusive term. The one which I find most appropriate and easily understood is 'Lifeskills'. It is an umbrella term for all our daily activities and incorporates all the skills mentioned above. I define Lifeskills as:

Those skills which enable a person to function as happily and independently as possible in his or her own environment.

Everything we do every day is therefore a Lifeskill. Most of these skills, once acquired, become automatic and we no longer acknowledge them as skills. Successful Lifeskills training depends to a large extent on the identification and evaluation of each individual skill.

Key point
In order to teach Lifeskills effectively, it is important to become aware of all the skills involved in what may seem to be a simple daily task.

Real Life Example

It is 7.30 a.m. John gets up, takes a quick shower and gets dressed. He makes his bed and goes downstairs. For breakfast he has a bowl of cereal, a cup of tea and toast. While eating, he listens to the 8 o'clock news.

John brings his mother a cup of tea in bed, then, at 8.30 he puts on his coat and leaves home to catch the bus to work.

This is a standard first hour of the morning for many people and it is simple for John.

Jane, however, cannot get up and dress herself independently in the morning. She needs to learn how to manage, as her mother, who has always helped her, is no longer able to do so due to poor health.

To achieve what John can do, which many of us would not rate as a major achievement, Jane would have to acquire all the following skills:

Functional numeracy —telling the time
Personal hygiene   —showering
Self-care   —dressing
Home skills   —making breakfast
Communication skills—speaking with mother and on the bus
Decision-making   —what to do next, what coat to wear, etc.
Community skills   —using public transport.

How does the instructor know how to separate these skills and then decide where to begin?

THE LIFESKILLS NETWORK

In this chapter, I shall examine the vast range of Lifeskills and divide them into comprehensive and easily understood categories. This structure is called the 'Lifeskills Network'. I have devised it over many years, correcting and refining it where necessary. I am now confident that it is logical, concise yet very comprehensive. It allows for tasks to be added under given headings and so adapts easily to suit individual needs. It will be a main source of reference throughout the book and hopefully of real value to instructors in future Lifeskills training. Correct use of the Network will be explained later in the book.

One of the most difficult aspects of teaching Lifeskills is knowing where to begin. It is common for both instructor and trainee to feel overwhelmed by the huge range of skills which the trainee requires for day-to-day living; there seems to be so much to learn that both parties feel helpless and despondent. The danger is that too much may be taken on too quickly, and the resulting training will only touch the surface of a range of skills but see no tangible or satisfying results.

Familiarity with the Lifeskills Network helps one to avoid falling into the trap of taking on too much.

Real Life Example

Let's return to Jane. As we saw, she cannot get up and dress independently in the morning and it is important that she learns these skills. An instructor set aside time to train Jane 'to become independent in the morning'. She began with personal hygiene. As they progressed, she realised that this was a much more complex skill than she had anticipated. She then realised that Jane did not know when to get up. She therefore began a new programme on clock skills and after some time realised that Jane did not know numbers. For a while they worked on numbers but both got bogged down and frustrated. They began afresh on dressing skills but as Jane could not differentiate between clean and dirty clothes, they abandoned dressing and looked at 'care of clothes'.

Six months later, having spent two mornings a week training, Jane could:

- Regulate the temperature on the shower.
- Identify the numbers 2, 3, 6 and 9.
- Identify the front and back of clothes by the label.
- Identify dirty clothes by sight only.

They had touched on a wide range of skills but Jane had only learnt a few disjointed bits and pieces. She still did not know when to get up and was not much closer to managing independently in the morning.

RESULTS: frustration for Jane and the instructor and worry for Jane's mother.

A better way
Jane's instructor studied the Lifeskills Network and examined the 'morning procedure'. She was amazed to

discover all the skills that were involved in simply getting up and out to work. Understanding the complexity of a seemingly simple procedure made the instructor approach the training in a much more confident and realistic way. She and Jane selected and agreed on the first goal:

- Teach Jane to get up at 7.30 a.m. independently, five mornings a week.

This did not necessitate Jane knowing how to tell the time.

Key point
Think creatively about problem-solving, always checking to see if there is a simple way around a problem.

Jane and her instructor enjoyed a trip into the city to select and buy a battery-operated alarm clock. The instructor set the alarm for 7.30 a.m. and then:

- Taught Jane how to pull up the button before going to bed.
- Familiarised Jane with the sound of the alarm.
- Explained that the alarm sound was the signal to get up.
- Taught Jane how to press down the button to turn off the alarm.
- Positioned the alarm clock in such a way that Jane would have to get out of bed to turn it off and would therefore be less likely to go back to sleep.

They put the plan into action with Jane's mother standing by in case anything went wrong.

RESULT—ACHIEVEMENT. Jane, her mother and the instructor are delighted. This is only one small step in the 'morning procedure' but it is a positive step and *achievement motivates* one for further skill acquisition.

Understanding the Lifeskills Network enables the instructor to approach Lifeskills training with greater clarity and confidence. This confidence filters through to the trainee, making the process of skill selection more efficient. Like using a menu, the instructor and trainee will be able to examine the whole selection of skills and then choose what they need.

There are other important factors in the process of skill selection, such as knowing the trainee well and analysing individual tasks: these will be addressed later in the book. But first let us concentrate on the Lifeskills Network.

How the Lifeskills Network operates

My aim in devising this network was to make it:

    Comprehensive—covering all skills
    Clear   —for easy reference
and *Logical*   —for easy understanding and retention.

The network is divided into three skill levels:

CORE SKILLS

which break down into

MAIN SKILLS

which break down into

INDIVIDUAL TASKS

There are six core skills which represent the main areas of daily life:

1	Self-care	4	Leisure skills
2	Home skills	5	Interpersonal skills
3	Community skills	6	Work skills

Each of these *core skills* covers such a range of activities that it is necessary to break them down into manageable divisions. I will call the first division *main skills*. For example:

CORE SKILL
SELF-CARE

MAIN SKILLS
Personal hygiene
Personal appearance
Self identification
Sexuality
Personal safety

Each main skill is further divided into numerous *individual tasks*, which are listed later in this chapter. These lists cannot claim to be complete as there are endless individual tasks, but they give an indication as to how the main skills break down and how each little daily activity has its place in the network.

The individual task division of the Network is intended to be flexible. This facilitates the selection of appropriate individual tasks from the given lists and the inclusion of others (identified by instructor or trainee) which have not been listed. As the instructor becomes more familiar with task analysis and the personalities of the trainees, she is likely to discover more individual tasks which need to be included.

Overlap
The division of skills into different sections is not absolute; there will be overlap and some skills can justifiably be entered in two or more sections. This should not cause confusion but simply emphasise different aspects of the one skill. For example:

Safety
Safety in the home   —Home skills
Safety in the community—Community skills
Safety at work   —Work skills
Personal safety   —Self-care

The Lifeskills Network
To make it as clear and easily understood as possible, the Lifeskills Network is explained in a series of diagrams. How to use the Network to the best advantage of both trainee and instructor is detailed in Chapter 3 and elsewhere throughout the book.

THE LIFESKILLS NETWORK

CORE SKILLS AREAS

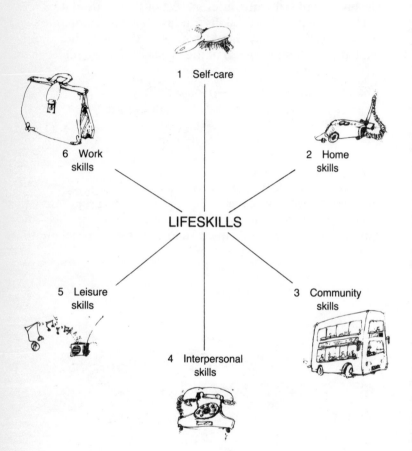

1   Self-care

6   Work
    skills

2   Home
    skills

LIFESKILLS

5   Leisure
    skills

3   Community
    skills

4   Interpersonal
    skills

1 SELF-CARE

MAIN SKILLS

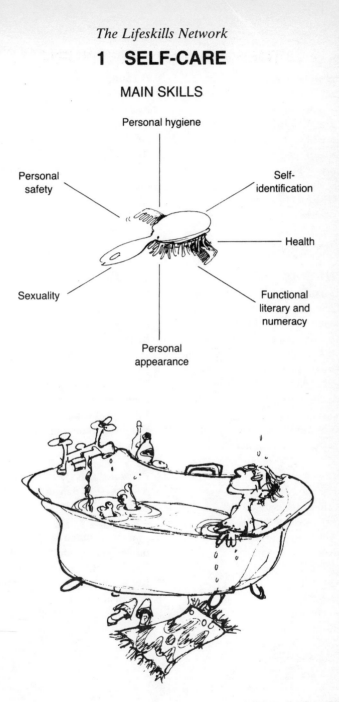

Personal hygiene

Personal safety

Self-identification

Health

Sexuality

Functional literary and numeracy

Personal appearance

SELF-CARE—Individual tasks

Personal hygiene
Care of skin
Care of hair
Care of hands
Care of feet
Care of teeth
Care of nose
Shaving
Menstrual hygiene
Toilet hygiene
Hygiene products
Hygiene routine

Personal appearance
Posture/gait
Facial expression
Grooming
Dressing
Buying clothes
Appropriate selection of clothes
Presentation/appearance of clothes
Checking one's weight
Using make-up
Fashion
Weight

Self-identification
Recognition of self/body image
Knowledge of body parts
Understanding of left and right
Knowing personal identity
—name, address, date of birth
Knowing own weight and height
Self confidence/assertiveness
Making choices
Having opinions
Knowing strengths and weaknesses
Having a value system

Sexuality
Knowing own gender
Male sexuality
Female sexuality
Body parts—male
                    —female
Facts of life
Reproductive system
Appropriate sexual behaviour
Safety/protection
Non-verbal communication

Health
How the body works
   (in suitable detail)
Diet → weight
Exercise
Sleep
Identifying illness
Self-help
Seeking help
Doctors/specialists
Hospitals and clinics
Minor injuries and ailments
Common illnesses
First aid

Personal safety
Awareness of dangers
   at home
   at work
   in the community
Implementing safety procedure
Dealing with emergencies
Reporting accidents/incidents
Anticipating danger
Prevention of accidents

Functional literary and numeracy
Colour
   Identification of colours
   Matching colours
Size, weight, measurements
Shoe and clothes sizes
Own size and measurements
Own weight/ideal weight
Reading labels and washing instructions/recipes and menus

2   HOME SKILLS

MAIN SKILLS

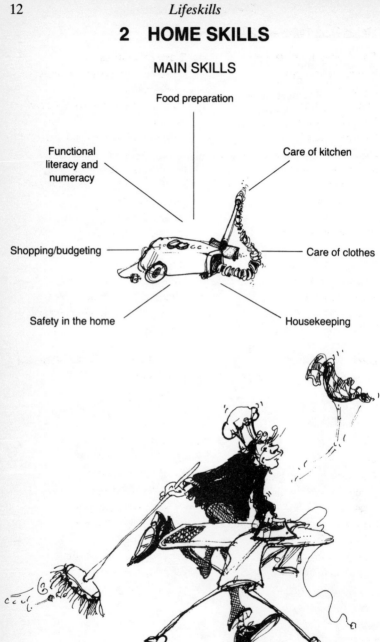

Food preparation

Functional
literacy and
numeracy

Care of kitchen

Shopping/budgeting

Care of clothes

Safety in the home

Housekeeping

HOME SKILLS—Individual tasks

Food preparation

Food types/origins
Balanced diet
Menu planning
Following a recipe
Storage of food
Kitchen utensils
Electrical equipment
    e.g. kettle
        mixer
        toaster
        cooker
        microwave
Planning the time
Preparing a snack
Preparing a meal
Hygiene while cooking
Safety while cooking

Care of the kitchen

Knowledge of the kitchen
   (orientation)
Identification of equipment
Cleaning products
Safety in the kitchen

Setting a table
Washing and drying dishes
Sweeping/washing the floor
Cleaning worktops
Cleaning cupboards
Cleaning the fridge
Cleaning the cooker
Disposal of rubbish

Dealing with problems/
   emergencies
Support services
Kitchen cleaning routine

Care of clothes

Differentiating between under/
   over clothes
Identifying signs of soiled/dirty
   clothes
Differentiating between different
   material types
Separating light/dark colours
Washing clothes—hand/machine
Drying clothes
Airing clothes
Storing clothes
Ironing clothes
Repairing clothes
Shoe care
Clothes care routine
When and how to use cleaners/
   launderette

Housekeeping (other than the kitchen)

Using the vacuum cleaner
Dusting
Polishing
Sweeping
Cleaning products
Removal of rubbish
Cleaning windows

Cleaning the bathroom
Cleaning the bedroom
Making a bed
Cleaning the living-room
Cleaning the stairs

Housekeeping routine

Safety in the home

Safety in the kitchen
Sharp objects
Spills
Electrical equipment
Cooker/hot surfaces
Bad food
Untidiness

Electrical safety
Plugs/fuses
Wiring
Repairs

Fire safety
Risks with smokers
Kitchen fires
Lighting fires
Using heaters
Smoke alarms
Fire extinguishers/procedures
Gas leaks
Flooding
Break-ins
Accident prevention and where to seek help

Security in the home
Locks
Alarms
Telephone
A safety routine
Bogus, other callers
Looking for identification
Door chain
Spy-hole

Shopping/budgeting

Knowing local area
Identifying types of shops
Stock-taking at home
Compiling a shopping list
Budgeting daily/weekly
Selection of food
Identifying fresh food
Use of money
Packing of food
Carrying shopping
Assertiveness
Seeking help
Safety with money
A shopping routine

Functional literacy and numeracy

Basic use of the telephone
Using the telephone in an emergency
Basic literacy
Writing a message
Writing a shopping list

Reading
Social sight vocabulary—signs/notices
Reading signs/notices

Time
telling the time
planning time
estimating length of time to complete a task

Money
Understanding of money for shopping

3 COMMUNITY SKILLS

MAIN SKILLS

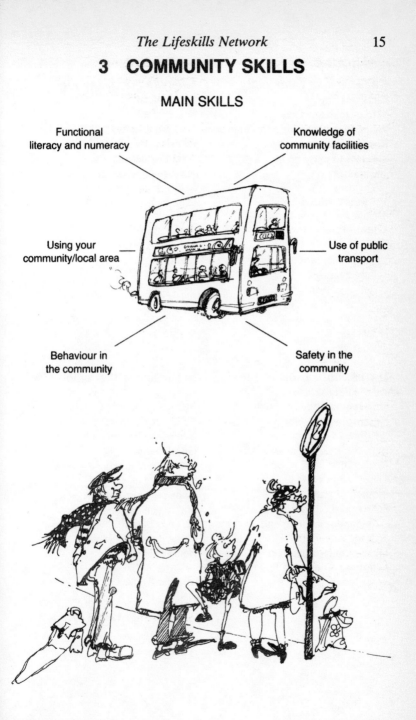

Functional
literacy and numeracy

Knowledge of
community facilities

Using your
community/local area

Use of public
transport

Behaviour in
the community

Safety in the
community

COMMUNITY SKILLS—Individual tasks

Knowledge of community facilities

Map of relevant area
Public transport within this area
Location of/how to use
  Places to eat
  Cinemas
  Theatres
  Sports facilities
  Colleges/classes
  Post office
  Bank
  Range of shops
  Public houses
  Police station
  Social Welfare Services
  Places of interest
  Library
  Churches

Safety in the community

Personal safety
Road safety
Care with money
Obeying the law
Avoiding getting lost
Awareness of danger
Safety measures
Seeking help
Saying 'No'
Basic safety rules
Impulse control
Making a phone call

Use of public transport

Road safety skills
Different methods of public
  transport
Routine on a bus/train
Behaviour on a bus/train
Recognition of numbers
Observation skills
Method of payment
Safety on the bus/train
Orientation, location and
  destination
Make enquiry/seek help
Following a bus/train timetable

Behaviour in the community

Behaviour on the bus
Behaviour in shops
Behaviour in 'quiet places'
Behaviour in public places
Good manners
How to queue up
How to be assertive
Knowing your rights
Making an enquiry
Behaving alone
Behaving with a group
Being friendly

Using your community/local area

Making arrangements
Planning time
Meeting people
Making choices
Finding information
Budgeting
Seeking permission
Varying activities
Making friends
Distinguishing between friends/
strangers

Functional literacy and numeracy

Use of the telephone
Private/public telephones/using a
call card

Time
Telling the time
Planning time
Making arrangements
Reading timetables

Concept of time
Days
Weeks
Months
Years
Seasons

Using money
Recognition of coins
Value of coins
Reading prices
Purchasing
Calculating change
Budgeting
Saving

Basic literacy
Social sight vocabulary
Reading signs, notices and menus
Writing own name and address

4　INTERPERSONAL SKILLS

MAIN SKILLS

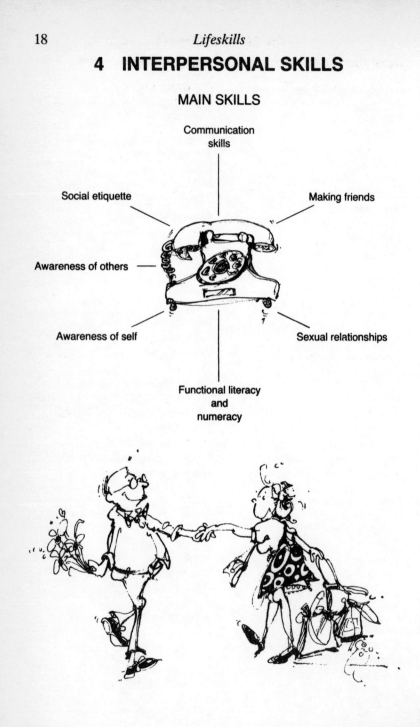

INTERPERSONAL SKILLS—Individual tasks

Communication skills

Non-verbal communication
Sign language
Eye contact
Posture
Physical distance
Facial expression
Picking up and giving social cues

Listening

Speech
Volume of speech
Content of speech
Clarity
Diction
Pronunciation
Tone

Making friends

Initiating conversation
Showing interest
Co-operating
Sharing
Shared activities
Making plans
Information sharing
Discussing likes and dislikes
Showing affection appropriately

Sexual relationships

Sexual knowledge
Sexual behaviour
Independence
Parental approval
Planning outings
Socially acceptable behaviour
Safety
Planning of time

Functional literacy and numeracy

Using the telephone
Letter writing

Awareness of self

Knowing likes and dislikes, strengths and weaknesses
Making choices
Knowing one's rights
Establishing realistic goals
Becoming confident
Being assertive
Knowing limitations
Identifying bad habits
Having a value system

Awareness of others

Identifying the needs of others
Showing consideration
Helping others
Avoiding others if necessary
Distinguishing between friends/ strangers
Picking up signals
Choosing people to be with
Accepting others

Social etiquette

Saying 'please' and 'thank you'
Queuing
Taking turns
Apologising
Facilitating others
Being punctual
Greeting others
Showing respect

5 LEISURE SKILLS

MAIN SKILLS

Home-based leisure

Functional
literacy and
numeracy

Planning leisure
time

Responsibility to
others

Friendship
skills

Community-based
leisure

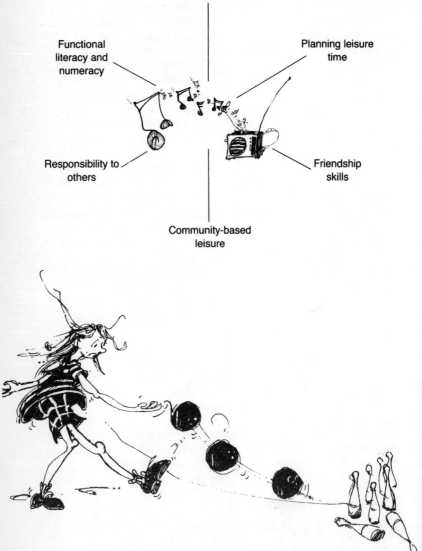

LEISURE SKILLS—Individual tasks

Home-based leisure

Developing hobbies:
  Arts and crafts
  Woodwork
  Card-playing
  Board games
  Computer games
  Music
  Reading
  Cookery
  Entertaining

Community-based leisure

Knowing local facilities:
  Sports
  Outdoor pursuits
  Cinema
  Theatre
  Eating out
  Shopping facilities
  Clubs
  Classes
  Places of interest
Using public transport
Geography of the area
Safety in the community

Planning leisure time

Understanding day, date, time
Making arrangements
Choosing activities—co-operation
Obtaining permission
Using a diary/calendar
Consulting appropriate people
Using the telephone
Introducing variety
Planning holidays

Responsibility to others

Allocating time to help at home
Leisure time with family
Visiting relatives and friends
Telling parents/those at home
  where you are and when you'll
  be back
Giving time/help to others (visiting
  sick/elderly)

Friendship skills

Honesty
Dependability
Interest in others
Ability to enjoy oneself
Initiative
Sharing
Co-operation
Including others
Loyalty

Functional literacy and numeracy for leisure

Reading
Finding out what is on locally
TV programmes
Social sight vocabulary
Reading notices
Reading for pleasure

Writing
Writing name and address
Writing a message
Letter writing

Numeracy
Use of money
Saving
Using the telephone
Recognising numbers
Counting

Time
Telling the time
Concept of time

6 WORK SKILLS

MAIN SKILLS

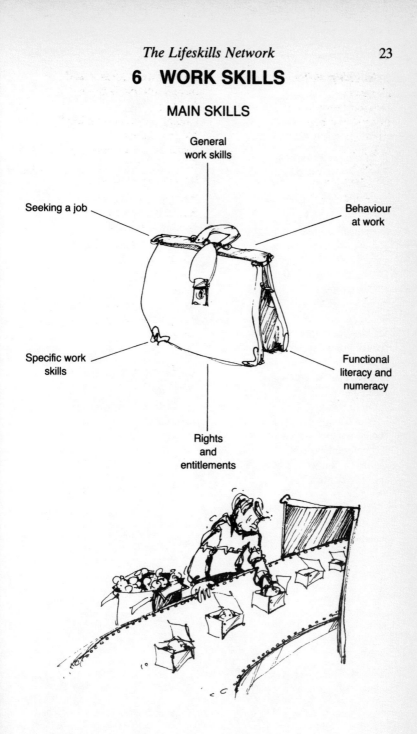

General
work skills

Seeking a job

Behaviour
at work

Specific work
skills

Functional
literacy and
numeracy

Rights
and
entitlements

WORK SKILLS—Individual tasks

General work skills
Concentration
Interest in work
Motivation
Retaining information
Ability to follow instruction
Speed of work
Accuracy of work
Task completion
Response to pressure
Using initiative
Care of tools
Understanding of safety
 procedures
Appropriate dress
Personal hygiene
Seeking help appropriately
Identifying mistakes

Rights and entitlements
Job description
Wages
Holidays
Sick leave
Conditions—space, heat, light etc.
Breaks
Disciplinary procedure
Union matters
Self-advocacy
Awareness of exploitation

Behaviour at work
Attendance
Time-keeping
Distractibility
Acceptance of criticism
Acceptance of discipline
Co-operation with others
Impulse control
Honesty
Socially appropriate behaviour
Relationship with staff
Relationship with co-workers

Specific work skills
Refer to:
 The task analysis of the
  particular job/jobs

Functional literacy and numeracy

Writing
Own name and address
Filling in a form

Time
Telling the time
Work hours

Concept of time
Days
Weeks
Months
Seasons

Size and measurement
Where appropriate to a job

Basic numeracy
Knowing the numbers
Counting
Adding, subtracting

Money
Understanding of money
Wages/budgeting

Seeking a job

Getting information
Newspapers
Agencies
Placement officer
Identifying own skills/preferences
Selling oneself
Filling out an application form
Interview skills
Starting a new job
Travelling arrangements
Rights and entitlements—see
    page 24

2   Know Your Trainee

It is vitally important for the instructor to have a real sense of who the trainee is—his personality, support system, strengths and weaknesses, and his hopes and dreams. A training programme should address the trainee's desires: only then will he be motivated to learn.

Key point
The trainee's motivation is an essential part of the learning process

Too often, random skills are taught and not retained because they were not needed or wanted by the trainee in the first place.

Real Life Example

Margaret is 25. She lives at home with her parents. Three days a week she works in a sheltered workshop and for the other two she works in a supermarket. Margaret's social outlets are very limited and, apart from work and the occasional family outing, she does not go out at all.

An enthusiastic member of staff in the workshop, who is the same age as Margaret and enjoys a busy social life herself, was horrified to think that Margaret had so little to do outside work. This instructor set time aside and put in a great deal of effort to alter this situation, working with Margaret to improve the quality of her social life. Over a period of three months, during work time and in her own time, the instructor:

- Took Margaret bowling and showed her how to play. She selected another trainee to come along to keep Margaret company.
- Took Margaret to the cinema and showed her how to

pay in and how to look up the films in the entertainment guide.
- Enrolled Margaret in a keep fit class as she was overweight and exercised very little.

When the three months were up and all activities had been practised, the instructor felt she should withdraw. She made a weekly timetable for Margaret to have at home, listing all the activities and starting times so that she could now continue on her own. The timetable looked great— Margaret's life was transformed . . . or was it?

During the first week, problems arose, the plan began to break down and Margaret was very disappointed.

What caused the breakdown?
- Margaret didn't get on with the woman who was selected to 'be her friend'. This was not obvious when the instructor was there, as she jollied the two of them along. When they went bowling alone they had a miserable game, neither one was interested in how the other was doing and they ended up having a row over the scores.
- Margaret was unable to use the bus independently, except on her route to work. The instructor hadn't realised this. Consequently, she was not able to get to the cinema on her own.
- The keep-fit class did not work either. Margaret was so nervous and conscious of her weight that she would not take off her coat when the instructor was not there to encourage and support her.
- Margaret got no encouragement from her mother to keep up the timetabled activities, as her mother felt that all this activity was too tiring and very expensive.

This is a very obvious case of the instructor not knowing the trainee. She did not set aside adequate time to get to know Margaret. She did not check out:

- Margaret's likes and dislikes, hopes and dreams.
- The skills Margaret had and what her needs were.
- Who were the important people in Margaret's life.
- What support Margaret would get from home for this venture.

The instructor made assumptions based on her own life, personality and tastes.

Weak spot

It is common for instructors to *think* that they know the individual trainee and that therefore they *know* what the trainee's needs are.

Knowing the trainee 'for years' is not a sound basis on which to make important decisions regarding his future. In fact, this familiarity can often lead to assumptions, generalisations and mis-information. Instructors seeking information on trainees should not depend on files or data which has been collected over the years. These can contain a lot of documentation but little *real information* on the trainee.

Just as useful information should be gathered on meeting a new trainee, so information on existing trainees should be examined at regular intervals for its relevance, and updated as necessary.

Real Life Example

Michael is 35 and has no brothers or sisters. His mother died three years ago and he lives with his father. His father has always been devoted to him, wanting to give him everything possible in life and protect him from any potential harm. As a result, he does everything for his son.

Michael has attended a sheltered workshop for 13 years, since he was 22. Over the years, he has worked at various aspects of the plastic packaging in which the workshop specialises. His favourite job is operating the shrink-wrapping machine and he does this very efficiently.

A placement officer was offering some work experience placements in the plastics industry, with a view to ongoing part-time employment. Michael was anxious to be considered, so the placement officer spoke with his father and his supervisor to get some background information. Following these two meetings, the placement officer wondered if Michael's father and his supervisor were both talking about the same person.

Summary of findings from Michael's father
- Michael is a pleasant boy, friendly and even-tempered, who causes no trouble.
- He can do very little himself, and needs help with everything.
- He is not safe to use any electrical equipment—he got an electric shock when he was nine.
- He shows no initiative and couldn't manage to look after himself without help.
- He cannot travel alone and was almost knocked down when they tried to train him to use the bus.
- He cannot handle money—but he doesn't need to.
- He does not adapt easily to change—he would be better off where he is.

Summary of findings from Michael's supervisor
- Michael is pleasant and friendly and very sociable.
- He is very independent in self-care skills—always clean, neat and tidy.

- He shows great initiative on the shop floor when materials run out or problems arise.
- He has a very good capacity to learn, picked up independent travel skills very quickly but seems to be over-protected at home.
- He is very anxious to move on and change—does not want to be 'here for ever'.

The father's impression of, and therefore approach to, Michael, is entirely different from that of Michael's supervisor.

Both have known him for years and think that they have the 'full picture'. In order to help Michael to progress in the direction in which he wants to go, an instructor would have to explore all aspects of Michael's life to help him establish a clear personal identity with which *he* is happy and which is accepted both at work and at home.

All trainees have individual backgrounds, personalities, needs and abilities which will affect their performance, interest and readiness to learn. It is essential that an instructor identifies these aspects of an individual before she can plan an individual training programme.

WHAT IS AN INDIVIDUAL TRAINING PROGRAMME?

It is the allocation of specific time, planned and agreed by instructor and trainee, to enable the trainee to develop the necessary knowledge and skills to reach his selected goals. Individual training programmes are the means by which a trainee-centred approach can be implemented. By adopting this type of approach, the instructor is acknowledging the trainee as an individual who can take an active part in planning his own future.

Some important features of an individual training programme
- Mutual respect between trainee and instructor.
- The trainee's interest and motivation.
- The trainee's active involvement in the planning of the programme.
- The trainee being allowed to progress at his own pace.

- The trainee being facilitated in using the style of learning which suits him best.
- The achievement of specific goals.

Key point
A training programme which is devised for general use, and not tailored to suit individual strengths and needs, is less likely to achieve specific results.

Accommodating individuals within groups

It is important to clarify that operating individual training programmes does not necessitate working on a one-to-one basis— few of us have that luxury. There is plenty of scope within a group setting to address a range of individual needs. The essential criterion is to take time to get to know and understand each person and to identify individual goals prior to drawing up the programme. Much of the content may be of benefit to the group as a whole; however, the programme must be designed to meet individual needs and acknowledge strengths.

Real Life Example

A group of five trainees all needed and wanted to learn how to use the telephone. Two group members needed this skill primarily as a safety measure in the community, and the others needed it more for security in the home. Two members did not have a telephone at home and another was not allowed to use the telephone at home.

The basic instructions for using the telephone were relevant to all five trainees, so the instructor carefully planned her training programme. Time was not allocated to getting to know the trainees individually or gathering the necessary information about them. Consequently, the instructor fell into the trap of making presumptions and generalisations. For example, having completed the first stage of the training programme, she said, 'We have now learnt how to use a private telephone. Could you all go home tonight and practise making a 'phone call to a friend.' The trainees' responses were:

'I don't have a 'phone.'

'I am not allowed to use the 'phone.'
'I don't have any friend to call.'

Having to give these responses in a group setting could cause embarrassment or feelings of inadequacy. This information should have been known by the instructor in advance. She could then have altered the instructions to accommodate the individual situations. ·

Key point
Individual differences can be accommodated within a group as long as they are known in advance.

INFORMATION GATHERING

In order to put a trainee-centred approach into operation the instructor must ask herself:
'Do I really know this trainee?'

Example
- What sort of background does this trainee have?
  —home
  —work
  —community
- What sort of personality does he have?
  —likes
  —dislikes
  —interests
  —temperament
- What are this trainee's strengths and needs?
- Who are the important people in his life?
- What sort of lifestyle does he have?
- What sort of lifestyle would he like to have?
- What opportunities does he have to make choices?

If the instructor has difficulty answering these questions or is unsure about the accuracy of her answers, then new information will have to be gathered.

Getting to know and understand the individual trainee, encouraging him to open up, discovering what *really* motivates him and makes him unique, is the process which really brings Lifeskills training to life!

Key point
Accurate, up-to-date information is an essential ingredient in the planning and provision of trainee-centred Lifeskills training.

Unless carried out efficiently, information gathering can be a long-drawn out and unproductive activity. Time can very easily be wasted if the procedure is haphazard or unfocused. Careful planning and preparation are required for successful information gathering. The instructor should not begin the process if she is:

- Unsure what information she wants.
- Unsure why she needs this information.
- Unsure how or where to get the information.
- Unsure what to do with the information when it is gathered.

Information gathering is sometimes seen as the 'soft option'—sitting down for a chat! This perception can cause an instructor to feel that she should apologise for giving time to what is, in fact, an essential process.

The often limited time allocated to Lifeskills training can cause instructors to feel that they must get on with training and be seen to *do* something rather than 'wasting' time gathering information. The truth of the matter is that training without really knowing the trainee will yield very poor results.

Key point
Training without adequate information puts both the trainee and the instructor on a training treadmill—using up a lot of time and energy and making a great effort, but getting nowhere.

The instructor must aim to find a balance between the information required and the time available to seek it out.

There are several ways of gathering information about an individual. The way which I have found to be most effective, time-efficient and respecting of the individual involves drawing up a *Personal Profile* and has been adapted from the work of John and Connie Lyle O'Brien. In their book *Framework for Accomplishment*, they stress that a key factor in training is to be familiar with the individual's interests, gifts, capacities and needs. They developed this method of building a detailed profile which they describe as 'a recording of an individual's whole life, past events, relationships, choices and ideas about a better future'.

The emphasis in drawing up a personal profile is to assist the trainee in thinking about himself and his future. He is encouraged to look at, and select to work on, some small but significant changes in his life. These should be within reach and, when achieved, should bring the trainee in the direction in which he wishes to go.

The personal profile gathers information by means of questionnaires and discussions with the trainee and others whom he has identified as being very important in his life.

The questionnaires, which are provided at the end of this chapter, can be used as they are or adapted by the reader. They provide, under six headings, a structure for the discussions which ensures that the trainee is kept firmly in focus and that all important aspects of his life are referred to.

Whether the reader is a parent who has known the trainee all his life, a new helper being introduced to the trainee for the first time, or a teacher who has several people's needs to consider, this systematic method of gathering information can be of great help.

STEPS IN DRAWING UP A PERSONAL PROFILE

1 Select the individual(s) whose profile you will be exploring

Offer that trainee an opportunity to stop and look at his life, what is happening currently and where his life is leading.

Explain what a personal profile is, how it is completed and how it would assist the trainee in thinking about his future. If, and only if, he understands and is happy to co-operate can the personal profile be completed.

2 Spend time with the trainee

Allocate specific and agreed time to get to know the trainee better through careful use of the given forms.

Assist the trainee in thinking about himself and generating ideas and suggestions about his future. Some trainees will require a great deal of prompting and encouragement to contribute any feelings or ideas; others will provide endless information which will have to be prioritised.

Create an atmosphere in which the trainee will feel relaxed and in command. Take time to clarify that *he* can provide all the information and that all the instructor can do is organise and document it with a view to making things happen.

It is common to have great difficulty getting information from people who have learning disabilities. This usually results from the fact that they have not had opportunities to contribute and make choices. There is often little evidence that their opinions have been valued—this becomes a vicious circle.

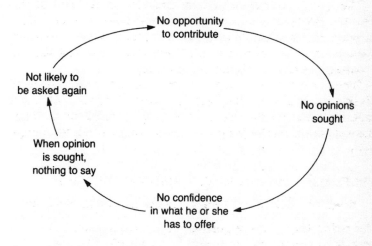

An individual's views, vision and openness are influenced by:
● The variety of experience and opportunities he has had.
● The type of service(s) he has received and over what period.
● The attitudes and opinions that family, friends and others have of him.
● His ability to express himself.
● The skills and resources he has and can use.

When looking for information from the trainee, do not give up easily. Probe carefully, wait patiently, gratefully accept any information at all—even one word—and capitalise on it.

Example

Instructor:	John, what do you enjoy doing on Saturdays?
John:	I don't know.
Instructor:	Do you have any hobbies or interests?
John:	No.
Instructor:	If your brother said he would bring you out any-where you would like, where would you choose?
John:	Anywhere. *(Do not give up yet.)*
Instructor:	Can you close your eyes and think of somewhere that makes you really happy?
John:	Aeroplanes.
Instructor:	Are you interested in aeroplanes?
John:	Oh yes, I went on a plane once. *(Respond to any spark of interest.)*
Instructor:	What about a trip to the airport?
John:	That would be great.

3   Meet and talk to other relevant people

In order to get a full picture of the trainee, it is necessary to get information from other people who play key roles in his life.

Find out who are the most important people in the life of the trainee. One way of doing this is to complete the 'circle of friends', an exercise taken from *Action for Inclusion* by Forest, Snow and O'Brien.

Ask the trainee to list all the people he knows—family, friends, neighbours, others, in no particular order. Then complete the circle of friends on a large sheet of paper:

In circle 1:   Put the names of the people closest to the trainee, people with whom he lives, is intimate with or depends on most.

In circle 2:   Put the names of the people whom the trainee really likes and has fun with, but who are not as close as those in circle 1.

In circle 3:   Put the names of others that the trainee knows through groups, clubs, work and so on.

In circle 4:   Put people who provide a service—doctor, dentist, shopkeeper, librarian and so on.

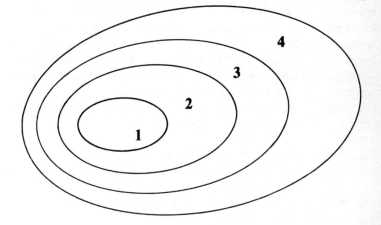

Real Life Example

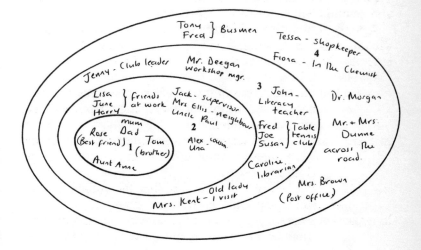

This exercise should help the trainee to think about the people in his life and identify those who are most important. I have found the visual aspect of the 'circle of friends' very helpful to trainees.

Make arrangements to meet and talk to the most relevant people, particularly those from circles 1 and 2. Explain the purpose of the meeting—to get as full and realistic a picture of the trainee as possible in order to plan and provide a programme of real value. Use the questionnaires given at the end of this chapter to keep the meetings efficient and the information to the point.

Some points to bear in mind when gathering information
1   Make sure that the trainee understands what is being done and gives his agreement.
2   Plan time carefully, agree times to see the relevant people and decide on the duration of each meeting.
3   Have a clear purpose in mind for each meeting, and explain this in a straightforward way which will be easily understood.
4   Decide on a suitable method of recording information at the meeting which is agreeable to the informant.
5   Be friendly, open and put people at ease.
6   Ask clear questions. How the question is phrased will determine the quality of the information given. Poor information will lead to a weak profile.
7   Accept all information: the role of the instructor is one of listening, not debating.
8   Avoid generalisations.
9   The profile is intended to reflect the trainee, therefore be careful not to impose your own ideas and values.
10 Give feedback. At the end of the meeting, summarise the main points to check that the information recorded is accurate. Give the informant some indication of when and how this information will be used.

4   Analyse the information gathered and make a summary

You may emerge from the information gathering stage with pages of information, stories and opinions. In successful profiling, the information gathered should make the trainee 'come alive', so it is necessary to prioritise the data.

You may come across *conflicting opinions*. Remember, there are no absolutes about a person's needs and you are not looking for a consensus. Ultimately, you will have to make a judgement on crucial issues where there is conflict.

Beware of hidden agendas and side-tracking; try to stick firmly to the information you are seeking. *Keep the trainee firmly in focus*.

In compiling the profile, you are helping the trainee to see new possibilities without imposing your own preferences.

Summarising

Together the trainee and the instructor should summarise the findings from the completed questionnaires, writing down the most important aspects of the individual's life under the given headings. A helpful way of doing this is by making a poster with the trainee's name in the centre and the headings spaced around the outside. Fill in the most important information under each heading, using pictures, words or short phrases.

This is a useful visual summary, particularly for trainees who have difficulties with literacy. It is called a *personal profile poster*, an example of which is given on page 48.

5 Use the information gathered to search for potential and build a vision of a worthwhile future

By reflecting on the information gathered and completing a summary, the trainee will see the various elements of his life come together, making up the whole picture of the present situation.

The role of the instructor is to assist the trainee in using this information to make decisions about the future. She should not be influenced by:

- Her own beliefs and values.
- What has been achieved before.
- The limits which others set on the student's capacity.
- The traditional approach to training in the workplace/home.

The future will come whether we plan for it or not. We can wait for it to arrive and do nothing, in which case others will determine largely how it will be. However, by engaging in vision-making, we can think about and prepare for the future and at least partially influence how it will be.

Vision-making requires imagination and creativity. It leaves behind the limitation of the present and allows us to be free to explore new possibilities.

We can be too bound up in what is 'realistic'. People need to dream and express what they hope for the future. There is benefit in dreaming and breaking through the existing boundaries of what is thought to be possible.

It is very common for people who have learning disabilities to feel tied down because of the great range of limitations which have been imposed on them. Many have learnt that it is not worth expressing their wishes or hopes, because they have never been listened to.

When creating a vision, you must listen carefully to the *desires* of the person. Encourage spontaneity and freedom of expression, and help the individual to focus on his potential and how this can be used to make the vision a reality. It may be only through this process that a chink of light will appear and the trainee's control of his own future begin.

Once the trainee has experienced the freedom to dream and express his desires for the future, the instructor can help him to focus on his potential, the available resources and how these can work together to make the dream become a reality.

Key point
Having an understanding of where the trainee wants to get to in life is an important prerequisite to developing a plan of action.

Some trainees will have wild flamboyant dreams while others will need great encouragement and support in expressing any dream at all. Whatever the expression, you must listen carefully and respectfully. Do not tell the trainee what is right or wrong, possible or impossible. Encourage him to be specific rather than generalising—'In five years time I want to work in open employment', rather than, 'In five years time I want to be happy.'

Real Life Example

Elizabeth is 30 and has lived in a group home for five years since her mother died. She attends a sheltered workshop every day, where she works hard and makes very few demands on others. In the group home she lives quietly, doing more than her fair share of household chores. She is the type of person who easily fades into the background, making so few demands that her needs are not often considered.

Having completed a personal profile with Elizabeth, the instructor was still unsure what her needs were or what direction her individual training programme should take. She worked with Elizabeth on making a vision for the future. Elizabeth said she had no dreams—just got on with life. The instructor was patient and encouraging, asking her a range of questions to provoke her to take some control of the future. Gradually Elizabeth began to verbalise her dreams, modest at first—'I would like to lose a stone in weight', 'I would like to decorate my bedroom', and other such dreams. Suddenly her face lit up and she said in a different tone of voice altogether: 'I would love to be a nurse.'

This was a turning point in Elizabeth's life. She did not become a nurse but she did a First Aid course, and was put in charge of First Aid at her work and her club. She joined the St John's Ambulance voluntary organisation, and she now attends weekly meetings and regular public events, where she assists in carrying out emergency First Aid. She has found a way to contribute to the lives of others and this sense of fulfilment has changed her whole personality.

By expressing a dream which was buried deep inside her, she gave the instructor the necessary indication of where she wanted to go.

Key point
By helping someone to establish a vision of what his or her future might look like, we change the way in which that individual thinks about him- or herself.

Vision making

To encourage a trainee to dream or develop a vision for his future, the instructor could ask questions, like:

1 Temporarily ignoring limits or restraints, how would you like your life to be in five years' time in the areas of:
   a) living arrangements?
   b) job situation?
   c) education?
   d) friendships?
   e) recreation?
2 What would you like most to change in your life?
3 If you could be anywhere in the world, where would you like to be?
4 If you won £100,000, what would you do?
5 If you could be anyone you wanted, who would you be?

6 If you could have anything you wanted, what would you choose first?

When you have a good understanding of the trainee and his hopes for the future, you can begin to develop a strategy to help him move in the direction in which he wants to go. This process, drawing up an individual training programme, is detailed in the following chapters.

THE PERSONAL PROFILE

Profile of: _____

People who contributed to the profile:

_____
_____
_____
_____
_____
_____

Trainee's background

What are the main aspects of the past which have shaped the present?

Date of birth?
How many in the family?
Trainee's position in the family?
Where did the trainee live, with whom and for how long?
Did he miss out on any typical experiences?
Where did the trainee go to school?
Was this a good experience?
Were friendships formed and did they last?
Does the trainee go to work?
How long is he in current work?
Did he have other work experiences?
What relationships has he developed?
Other important information

Personality

What are the trainee's abilities and interests?
What does the trainee like doing best?
What else does he enjoy?
When is the trainee both relaxed and comfortable?
When is the trainee bored?
What does the trainee spend most of the day doing?
What does he spend most of his leisure time doing?
Does the trainee initiate change/development in his own life?

What contribution does the trainee make to the lives of others?

What are the trainee's greatest strengths?

What are the main features that make this trainee unique?

Does the trainee have any idea of his own potential?

Important people

Who are the people most involved in this trainee's life?

What contribution do they make, or what effect do they have, on the life of the trainee?

Parents—relationship with them in the past

Relationship with parents now

Relationship with other family members in the past

Relationship with other family members now

Did any members of the extended family (aunts, uncles, cousins, etc.) play an important role in the past?

Are they involved now?

Who does the trainee spend most time with every day/week?

Does the trainee like/get on with the people at work—staff/peers?

Are there any important people whom the trainee sees occasionally?

Who are the trainee's closest friends, in whom he can confide and trust?

Has any special person been lost by the trainee through death, distance or disharmony?

Lifestyle

How does the trainee spend his time?

What does the trainee do on—
   a daily basis?
   a weekly basis?
   occasionally?

What activities does the trainee partake in—
   alone?
   in a small group?
   in a large group?

Are there activities which the trainee would like to partake in, but for some reason does not?

What community facilities does the trainee avail himself of?
  e.g. shops, bank, library, cinema
What means of transport does the trainee use?
Does the trainee go on holidays?
Has he ever travelled abroad?
Does the trainee have access to personal money?
Are there restrictions on the trainee's freedom?
What does the trainee enjoy doing most?
What does the trainee like doing least?

Role in life

What roles does the trainee occupy?
  e.g. worker, helper/child
How have these roles changed over the years?
Are these roles valued socially?
What would other community members see this trainee
  doing?
How would they describe this trainee?
What characteristics of the trainee would contribute to a
  positive reputation?
What characteristics of the trainee would contribute to a
  negative reputation?
How is the trainee's dignity supported with regard to privacy
  and personal possessions?
Does this trainee have the opportunity to make choices?
What language and labels are used by professionals to de-
  scribe the trainee?
Does this trainee make any decisions for himself?
Does this trainee make any decision with the support of
  others?
Do others make decisions for this trainee?

Needs

What problems does the trainee face and what help would he
  benefit from?
What situations pose the greatest challenge to this trainee?
Are there practical problems which he faces on a daily/weekly
  basis?
With which area of his life is he most dissatisfied?

Who or what provides the most practical help?

What are the greatest barriers to progress—
    at home?
    at work?
    in the community?

Does he require any special support with health-related issues
    e.g. mobility/hearing/speech/epilepsy?

What skills has this trainee learnt most recently?
    How were these learnt?
    Where?
    With the help of whom?

Lifeskills

PERSONAL PROFILE POSTER

Date: _____

Personality

Background   Important People

Focus Person

Name: _____

Date of birth: _____

Lifestyle   Needs

Role in Life

PERSONAL PROFILE POSTER

Date: 10·2·'94

Personality

Quiet, gentle
worries a lot

Hates fights

Fussy about
things being
clean and tidy

loves animals

Focus Person

Name: Julie Brown

Date of birth: 20·1·'69

'I would be a
good friend to
someone but I
don't know where
to start'

Background

Youngest in the
family

Very loving family ♡

Never goes out
without a
family member

Never spent a
night away
from home.

Does not look
after own
money £££

Important People

Mum
Dad
Sally (sister)
Colin (brother)
Jackie (sister in law)
Emma + Ruth (niec
Bert (supervisor
Molly (elderly
              neighbour

Lifestyle

Lives at home
with mum, Dad
and older sister Sally

Works in a sheltered
workshop

Stays in a lot and
watches T.V.

Never gets a letter
or a phone call

Role in Life

Adult

Dependable
        worker

Babysitter

Minds the
pets

Needs

Friends

Somewhere to go

More fun in Life

To become more
independent of
        family

New hobbies
and interests

3 Agreeing Goals And Selecting Skills

The importance of well-informed skill selection, and firm agreement on specific and realistic goals, cannot be emphasised enough.

In this chapter I want to show how familiarity with the range and breakdown of Lifeskills (Chapter 1), knowledge of and respect for the individual (Chapter 2) and a range of other considerations will come together in the successful selection of skills and identification of goals for any trainee. If this procedure is followed, the training process will almost certainly yield positive, tangible results. It may appear as though a process which has been relatively quick and straightforward in the past—that is, an instructor selecting a skill which she *thinks* would benefit an individual or group—will now become long and involved. At first, the collection of information and negotiation with the trainee will be time-consuming, but as a bank of accurate information is gathered it will only require updating at agreed intervals. As trainees become more confident and adept at sharing information and making choices, the whole procedure will become more efficient and streamlined. When training programmes genuinely address a trainee's needs and wishes, he will be better motivated to participate and progress will be evident.

> **Key point**
> *Energy is used constructively in the preparation of a training programme rather than wasted on continuous training which has no specific goal.*

As stated by Priestley *et al* in *Social Skills and Personal Problem Solving*, movement towards goals of any kind must start with an awareness of some personal need and a desire to do something about it. People are hardly ever motivated to solve problems which have been defined for them by others. It is essential, therefore, that the needs being addressed should be those seen and expressed by the individual.

Does the following scenario ring a bell?

Real Life Example

Philip is 38. He attends a sheltered workshop where the light engineering unit assembles components for the computer industry. Philip is good at his work but because of its repetitive nature he becomes bored and makes a lot of mistakes.

Philip's supervisor has been bothered for some time by the fact that Philip's personal hygiene leaves a lot to be desired, and in particular he has very smelly feet. He refers this matter to the training officer, who looks over some rather dated information about Philip's background and sees that he lives with 'elderly parents in fairly difficult circumstances'.

Someone worked with Philip three years ago on his general hygiene. They left a note in his file to say, 'Following a three-month training programme in self-care, there is a great improvement in Philip's personal hygiene'. The training officer decides that Philip needs some re-training. He calls Philip in for a chat.

Training Officer:	Hello, Philip, how is work going?
Philip:	Ah, it's going fine. A bit boring, but that's life, isn't it?
Training Officer:	Well, Philip, I think it's time we took another look at your personal hygiene—do you know what that means?
Philip:	Yeah, baths.
Training Officer:	Yes, baths are part of the process, but I would like to concentrate first on your feet.
Philip:	What about them?
Training Officer:	Well, if feet are not properly looked after they can start to smell.

Philip:	My feet don't smell!
Training Officer:	I'm not saying they do, but what about doing some work together on the hygiene of feet, just in case there is room for improvement?
Philip:	All right, I don't mind.

The training officer works with Philip two days a week for a month. He puts in a lot of time and effort and is disappointed that Philip is not more co-operative or better motivated. When the programme is finished there is a noticeable improvement in the condition of Philip's feet. The supervisor who raised the problem is delighted. However, over the next months Philip slips back into his old ways and the training is forgotten.

The training officer could say that he consulted Philip, discussed the issue with him and got his agreement. Was that really the case?

- Did Philip really have any say in the matter?
- Was the programme set up to meet Philip's needs or the supervisor's needs?
- Did the programme move Philip any closer to his goal?
- What was Philip's goal anyway?

Learning is possible without the trainee's consent—so is brainwashing! Learning is likely to last longer and take deeper root when the trainee concerned has freely chosen to co-operate with the proceedings, has formulated his own goals and pursues them in an organised and willing way. Sometimes it is necessary for a trainee to learn a particular skill in which he has little interest or perhaps even resents. The case of Philip's hygiene is a good example of this. In such situations the instructor should make every effort to help the trainee to understand the importance of the skill for him and see it in relation to his chosen goal. Then he will be motivated to learn. *Voluntary participation* is in fact the lynch pin of the guidelines for selecting a skill and agreeing a goal, which are set out in this chapter.

HOW TO AGREE GOALS AND SELECT SKILLS

1 Refer to the trainee's personal profile

The personal profile (see Chapter 2) should have identified some key features of the trainee's personality and important background information regarding his strengths, needs, potential and dreams for the future.

This up-to-date information and perception of the student, as a unique person with a lot to give and a lot to learn, is an essential ingredient in selecting a skill.

2 Involve the trainee in the process

Look at the personal profile with the trainee and together summarise the information you have gathered. Ask the trainee what he would like to choose as a first goal. The trainee may suggest a goal which seems unattainable or unrealistic, but *no matter how unrealistic it seems, always use the trainee's suggestion or incorporate it in the plan.*

For example, Susan, a trainee who is overprotected at home, doing nothing for herself, suggests: 'I want to move in to a flat.'

A common response to such a statement might be: 'Oh, that's out of the question,' or, 'Be realistic—you can't even make a cup of tea.'

Instead, the initiative should be acknowledged: 'So you want to move into a flat? Perhaps first we should aim to set up an independent living arrangement within our own home. Let's make that a long-term goal. In the meantime, there are a lot of skills which have to be learnt in order to move towards that goals.' Refer with Susan to the Lifeskills Network.

3 Use the Lifeskills Network

When selecting a skill and agreeing a goal, it is important to focus on groups of related skills which lead to a common goal (see Chapter 1) rather than picking skills at random. For example, it could be confusing to train an individual in the following way, over a period of a month:

Week 1. Goal: To put on his own socks.

Week 2. Goal: To butter a slice of bread.
Week 3. Goal: To look at a person when talking to him or her.
Week 4. Goal: To count up to 5.

These are valuable skills and the trainee may be anxious to learn them, but where are they leading?

> **Key point**
> *Individual skills should link together to bring the trainee in the direction in which he or she wishes to go.*

How to use the Lifeskills Network when agreeing goals and selecting skills

a   Core skills
With the information gathered in the personal profile, select one core skill area which clearly relates to the trainee's wishes for his future.

b   Main skills
Examine how that core skill area breaks down into a series of main skills. The trainee's needs and capacities may require him to work on several main skills. Prioritise the trainee's needs with his help and select one main skill with which to start.

c   Individual tasks
Each main skill is further broken down into a series of individual tasks. The lists of individual tasks given in Chapter 1 is not intended to be exhaustive as there are endless individual tasks, but it indicates how main skills break down. The instructor and trainee should examine this list and select from it or, with the trainee's particular needs firmly in focus, identify other individual tasks. One individual task should be selected with which to begin.

d   Task analysis
Analyse the chosen task, breaking it down into its most basic elements (see Chapter 4). Organise these into a simple and logical series in order that the task can be learnt as efficiently as possible. The instructor can then identify what the trainee

can do already, in order to establish a starting point and agree a goal.

4 Identify long-, medium- and short-term goals

In order to keep the instructor and the trainee focused and clear about where the current step is leading, the whole training programme is punctuated with goals. These provide opportunities for success and praise which in turn boost motivation.

A long-term goal on its own is too distant and out of reach. It may fade from view in the long training process and cause trainee and instructor to lose heart. For this reason I have introduced medium- and short-term goals.

Identifying goals clearly
Having decided on a goal, it must be defined carefully and written down as a clearly understandable plan of action. A clear goal shows:

Who (the trainee)
will do what (the task)
under what conditions (the circumstances)
to what degree of success (the criterion)
with what result (the motivator)
in what length of time (time plan).

When these elements are stated as part of the goal, the people involved are quite clear about what they are setting out to achieve. Identify each element in the examples that follow.

a   The long-term goal
This relates to the trainee's dream for the future. It is the focus which motivates the trainee and should be kept in sight. *The long-term goal should point to one core skill area.*

To refer back to Susan's dream (page 53): 'I want to move into a flat'. The instructor, having completed Susan's personal profile and met her parents, knows she would have little success in making this dream become a reality. He congratulates Susan on expressing this clear dream for the future and suggests that they use it as a basis on which to establish *a clearly defined long-term goal*: for example, in two years' time Susan will be living independently in a bedsitting-room within her parents' house. She will make her own light meals and snacks and entertain her friends. She will be responsible for the tidying and cleaning of her bedsitting-room. This long-term goal points Susan and her instructor towards the core skill 'Home Skills'.

b The medium-term goal

This refers to a major step in the direction of the long-term goal. There may be a number of medium-term goals to tackle on the way to the long-term goal. To help to establish the medium-term goals required, the instructor and trainee should refer to the main skills listed under the selected core skill area. For example:

Core skill—home skills
Main skill—housekeeping

A clearly defined medium-term goal would be:

By . . . . (date) Susan will identify the housekeeping skills necessary to live independently in a bedsitting-room, learn them one by one and, as each is learnt, build it into the daily/weekly routine at home.

Another example for Susan could be:

Core skill—home skills
Main skill—food preparation

By . . . . (time) Susan will be able to prepare breakfast and a selection of four simple, nutritious light meals. She will prepare evening meals for her parents and herself at the weekends.

c The short-term goal

This is the *here and now*, a tangible goal within easy reach. The trainee and the instructor must at all times keep the short-term goal in sight. There will be several short-term goals to tackle on the way to the medium-term goal.

The short-term goal is an individual task identified as a priority from the breakdown of a main skill. While working on an individual task the trainee should be clear about how it relates to the medium- and, ultimately, the long-term goal. In relation to

Susan's first medium-term goal (housekeeping), a short-term goal might be:

> By . . . . (date) Susan will know how to make a bed and do it each morning at home.

Another example of a short-term goal might be:

> By . . . . (date) Susan will know how best to store food in a fridge to ensure maximum hygiene and safety.

The short-term goal or individual task is analysed to establish the simplest steps by which it can be mastered (see Task Analysis, Chapter 4).

Summary: using the Lifeskills Network to establish long-, medium- and short-term goals

a   Identify the **core skill** which relates closest to the trainee's hopes for the future.   →   **define a long-term goal**

b   Prioritise and select the **main skill** which relates most closely to the trainee's needs.   →   **define a medium-term goal**

c   Prioritise and select an **individual task** with which to begin the training process.   →   **define a short-term goal**

> **Key point:**
> *Ensure that the trainee can see how the short-term goal relates to the medium-term goal which in turn relates to the long-term goal, the trainee's dream.*

5   Prompt the trainee where necessary

In the selection of a skill and the identification of a goal, it may seem as though the trainee is required to do a lot of soul-searching and initiate a lot of responses. You will know many who have not yet developed such abilities. The whole process has to be adapted to suit the individual trainee and some will require considerable prompting. However, you must work to ensure their active involvement in the process and resist the temptation to put words in their mouths.

Real Life Example

Instructor:	Niall, we have taken a good look at the type of person you are and the type of life you lead, and I certainly feel I know you much better now. What would you most like to do in the future, next year or the year after that?
Niall:	I don't know.
Instructor:	What sort of work would you enjoy?
Niall:	The same.
Instructor:	Is there anything you would like to change in your work?
Niall:	No.
Instructor:	As you get older and more independent, where would you like to live?
Niall:	At home with my Mum and Dad.
Instructor:	Have you any plans for when your Mum and Dad become old?
Niall:	My sister will mind me.
Instructor:	You said that you enjoyed watching TV and listening to tapes, would you like to have more to do in your spare time?
Niall:	Ah no, I'm OK.

(The instructor is finding it difficult to get any lead as to Niall's hopes and dreams and consequently cannot select a long-term goal. He will have to probe further and encourage Niall to dream, in the hope of identifying some flicker of interest to explore.)

Instructor:	Niall, if you won lots of money, what would you buy?
Niall:	I don't know.
Instructor:	Well, close your eyes for a moment and think of a lovely big bright shopping centre, with lots of shops. Now, can you think of something you might buy?

Niall: I would buy a present for my Mum.
Instructor: That's very kind of you. Why would you buy your mother a present?
Niall: She's good to me. She brings me on holidays.
Instructor: Do you like holidays?
Niall: Yes, I love holidays. We went on a boat once.

(The instructor notices a change in Niall's voice. It has brightened up and he is speaking in a more animated way.)

Instructor: Have you ever been on a plane?
Niall: No.
Instructor: Would you like to go on a plane?
Niall: Yes, I'd love to but I can't go on my own and I don't have any money.
Instructor: Well, let's write that down as a dream and look at what we could do to work towards it.

(At least, now, the instructor has a lead and most importantly he has Niall's interest. They identify the core skill—*leisure skills*—*and from this identify the* main skills *such as friendship skills and planning leisure time.)*

Key point
Probe and prompt until you see a chink of light, then explore this to the full.

Negotiation
With trainees who can express their thoughts and dreams more easily, the instructor should enter into negotiation in selecting a skill and identifying a goal.

Before a person can negotiate, he or she has to experience basic opportunities to choose. Parents of adults with learning disabilities may have to learn to overcome the habit, acquired over the years, of making decisions and choices for them. This practice may have been appropriate and necessary in childhood, but now it is time to encourage their son or daughter to make his or her own choices and decisions.

Negotiation involves the shifting from an essentially child/ adult relationship, where the balance of power is with the adult, to a more equable distribution, such as should exist between adults. Deciding what is negotiable, and gradually expanding this as trainees progress, is probably the best approach. There is no point in swamping trainees with opportunities to negotiate before they are able to avail themselves of them.

6   Ensure that the goal is realistic

Dreams and aspirations do not have to be realistic, in fact they are often created out of the temporary removal of all barriers, confines and limitations. Out of these dreams, the instructor must help the trainee to establish realistic goals in order to avoid disappointment.

Real Life Example

Rachel is 26. She is the youngest of three children. Over the past three years she has been involved in, and shared the excitement of, her two sisters' weddings. Although she thoroughly enjoyed both occasions, they did make her reflect on her own life and this made her feel very lonely.

When Rachel and her instructor had completed her personal profile, the instructor asked Rachel what dreams she had for the future. Without hesitation, Rachel replied that she wanted to have a boyfriend and get married.

The instructor congratulated Rachel on expressing such a clear goal. She explained that this was a very common dream, though unfortunately not something concrete that could be 'organised' and, for a range of reasons, not always possible. The instructor suggested, however, that Rachel, with her dream in mind, could start to build a much more interesting social life. This would allow her to mix with a wide selection of males and females of her own age, with whom she might form new friendships.

The realistic goal was:

Over the next year, Rachel would become involved in three social activities, one sport, one social club and one class, through which she would meet a range of new people.

This was clearly a move in the direction of her dream and yet it was realistic.

In order to select a realistic goal, the instructor and trainee have to consider:

- The resources available.
- The limitation imposed by work/home/community.
- The views/support of others directly affected.

7   Select skills which can be used immediately by the trainee

Learning a skill is only half the battle, retaining it is the other half. For all of us, skills fade very easily if they are not used; consequently the time and effort of instructor and trainee are wasted.

Real Life Example

Diana travels to work daily on a special bus. It was agreed by her and those who work with her that she had the ability to travel independently on public transport. Diana's long-term goal was, by the end of the year, to be able to visit the married members of her family, independently, on her way home from work, two days a week. Learning to use the bus independently, to and from work, was agreed as a medium-term goal.

This main skill (use of public transport) was broken down into individual tasks, through which Diana and her instructor worked one by one. Finally, Diana could travel the route alone with confidence.

However, Diana's mother had not been adequately consulted. She was delighted for her daughter to *learn* how to use the bus but she did not want her to lose the special door-to-door transport facility. This would happen if Diana put the skill to use on a daily basis. Diana's mother suffered from high blood pressure and said that she could not cope with the additional worries that independent travel would bring.

In a very short time Diana lost the skill of travelling independently to and from work.

The implication of this skill acquisition were not fully considered. So, although successfully acquired, the skill could not be put to use. Consequently, a lot of time and energy were wasted.

Key point
Skills fade quickly if they are not put into immediate use.

8 Do not take on too much

This is one of the most common stumbling blocks in Lifeskills training. Frequently, an instructor is confronted with such an array of needs, and wants so much to see progress, that she is inclined to suggest unrealistic goals.

The result is that the goal is not reached in the specified time and both instructor and trainee become disillusioned.

Real Life Example

Richard is the eldest of a family of four. He works in a sheltered workshop five days a week. His sister works in a shop and goes to night classes to improve her reading and writing.

Richard thinks that his sister is already great at reading and writing and would love, more than anything, to be able to read and write himself. So far he can only write his name.

Richard made his wishes known to the staff at the workshop. Nothing was done for some time. Richard persisted. One of the instructors then agreed to work with him two mornings a week between September and Christmas. The goal was: Richard would learn how to read and write.

- They began working on the way Richard formed his letters, in order to improve the way he wrote his name.
- Then they worked on writing his address, taking it one line at a time.

This process took much longer than Richard or his instructor had anticipated. By Christmas Richard was able to write his name and address independently, in an adult way—but that was all. Both Richard and the instructor were disappointed. Richard was still a long way from 'being able to read and write'.

Actually, they had made considerable progress which neither person acknowledged. The scenario would have been completely different if they had begun by recognising that the goal which they set was, in fact, a long-term goal. They could then have set realistic medium- and short-term goals to suit the available time.

9   Check out the requirements of the selected skill

Before deciding on a particular skill and defining a short-term goal, the instructor should consider the requirements of this skill:

a   in order to learn it.
b   in order to put it into practice.

a   *In order to learn a skill*
Consider the following resources:

TIME. How much time would it take to learn this skill? At what intervals should instruction take place? Is that time available? When allocated, does it clash with any other important activity? Are both instructor and trainee available at that time?

SPACE. Where would the training sessions take place? Would the location suit the skill and is the location available when required? For example, if the skill is most appropriately taught in the community, is it possible for the instructor and trainee to spend time in the trainee's community?

MATERIALS AND EQUIPMENT. What materials and equipment would be necessary to teach this skill? Are they available? If not, can they be acquired? The instructor should ensure that the necessary equipment is in good repair and not being used by others at the desired time.

FINANCE. Would the teaching of this skill require any financial backing? For example, a cookery session would require money to purchase ingredients, so the source and availability of this money should be clarified in advance.

EXPERIENCE. Would the teaching of the selected skill require particular experience? Is that experience available? For example, teaching the use of a particular machine may require experience in using that machine. Is someone available to share that experience?

INFORMATION. Would the teaching of this skill require any specific information? If so, what is the source of this information? For example, a community resource session may require details of the facilities in a particular community. Is this information available? Where can it be found?

PERMISSION. This may be required to use any of the above-mentioned resources. Instructor and trainee should seek permission appropriately and in advance of the training programme, to ensure that there are no misunderstandings and that no time is wasted.

b   In order to put the skill into practice

Once the skill has been acquired, the instructor should check the same list of resources to anticipate any new requirements which the trainee may now have. Let's assumed that the trainee has completed the training programme for the skill of having a bath independently three nights a week. In order to put this skill into practice, he will require:

- Parental permission, support and trust.
- Hot water to be made available at the agreed times.
- Access to soap, shampoo, sponge, towels and so on.
- Clean clothes to be made available.

All the requirements of a new skill should be checked in advance to avoid disappointment during or after the training programme.

10   Think creatively about required skills

Once the instructor and trainee have identified a skill which the trainee requires in order to progress as he wishes, they should examine the skill to find the simplest way around it.

Real Life Example

Andrew wanted to be able to get up and dress independently in the mornings so that he could call at a friend's house and they could travel to work together. He had always had to wait until his father got up to help him to shave, button his clothes and tie his shoelaces.

Andrew had been working very hard with his mother to

become independent in these skills. He mastered the shaving and buttoning but he could not manage his shoelaces. His mother analysed the task and made it as simple as she could, but Andrew could not grasp it.

Andrew spoke to his instructor at work, asking if she knew any easy ways to tie shoelaces. The instructor suggested that Andrew could buy shoes with Velcro fastenings instead of laces. She told him that these shoes were easily available in a range of colours and styles. The next pair of shoes Andrew bought had Velcro fastenings and he never had to have a shoelace tied again.

Key point
Always check to see if there is an easy way round a difficulty before investing a lot of time in teaching a skill.

When a skill has been selected and a short-term goal identified, two questions should always be asked:

1 What difference will this skill make in the life of the trainee?
2 What is the skill leading on to?

If the process of selecting a skill and agreeing a short-term goal has been carried out carefully, these questions will be answered easily and with conviction.

4   Know The Task Yourself

For many of us, Lifeskills are the tasks we do automatically every day. For this very reason, they can be difficult to teach. For example, to be able to tie your shoelaces is one thing; to be able to explain clearly to another person how it is done is an entirely different matter.

> **Key point**
> *Teaching Lifeskills is not simply a case of 'I can do it, so I can teach it'.*

In Chapter 1 of this book we examined the Lifeskills Network. This network illustrates how numerous and complex the skills of daily living are. It explains how a *core skill* breaks down into a range of *main skills*, which further divide into countless *individual tasks*.

This chapter explains how to focus on *individual tasks* in even more detail and break them down into their simplest elements.

In order to teach a task successfully to another person, the instructor must know that task in detail, have broken it down into its simplest elements and have established what the trainee already knows and what he needs to learn. This applies regardless of:

- what the task is
- who is teaching it
- where it is being taught.

If this procedure is not carried out, this is what can happen:

Real Life Example

Jane is 20, living at home with her parents and a younger sister. Jane attends a vocational training centre where she is learning a range of horticultural skills.

At a recent individual planning meeting in Jane's centre, the most important people to Jane, both at home and at work, gathered to assist her in some forward planning. It was suggested that her general performance both at home and at work was considerably below her capacity.

This made Jane defensive. She disagreed, saying that she was doing her best. It was not until it was explained as a compliment, 'we think you could do better than that', that Jane was prepared to think about the suggestion. She became more open and happy about the idea of becoming independent, particularly when her mother referred to the dream Jane had identified, of living independently by the time she was 30. This formed her long-term goal.

Setting goals

Over the following weeks, some new goals were agreed for Jane, both at home and at work.

The medium-term goal was:
Over the next six months, Jane will become involved in the household cleaning routine. She will take responsibility for four tasks—washing dishes, vacuuming, cleaning the bathroom and ironing, as detailed on a rota.

The first short-term goal was:
Jane will learn to wash the dishes at home in the evening over a period of a month. She will then take turns with her sister to wash the dishes after dinner. Jane's mother (Mrs Smith) will provide the instruction.

The training programme

Mrs Smith knows this task like the back of her hand and thinks it will be simple to teach. She gives the instructions:

1 'Gather up all the dishes, stacking the same sort of ones on top of each other.'

She leaves Jane to carry out step 1. When she returns, she sees that Jane has stacked up the dishes but has not removed the scraps of food. The dishes are stuck together with squashed food and sauces. The cups have been stacked without being emptied, causing the dregs of tea to spill over the rims.

Mrs Smith: Oh, Jane, you never scraped off the scraps of food. You *know* you have to do that first.

Jane: You only told me to stack the dishes.

(This leads to confusion, negative feedback, loss of confidence and extra work. They start again.)

1   Scrape the plates and empty the cups down the sink.
2   Stack the dishes with similar ones on top of each other.
(Jane completes the first two steps successfully, then Mrs Smith introduces step 3.)
3   Fill the sink with hot soapy water. Put a few dishes in at a time.
(Jane fills the sink so full that when she puts the dishes in it overflows. She mops the floor with the dish cloth and continues. She washes the greasy plates first, which means that the cups and glasses, left to the end, are smeared with grease.

Mrs Smith returns. She sees the wet floor and the greasy cups.)

Mrs Smith: You put too much water in the sink, and didn't I tell you to do the cups and glasses first?

Jane: No, you didn't tell me and I'm not going to wash dishes ever again.

(Jane storms off in a rage.)

Results:

- Breakdown of the training programme.
- Loss of motivation.
- Negative feelings for Jane and Mrs Smith.
- Reinforcement of dependency.
- Mother's despair—'she'll never learn'.

This training programme failed almost before it began. Its failure had nothing to do with Jane's ability or how well her mother knew the task. *It failed because the task was not carefully examined and therefore the instructions were not clear.*

When teaching an everyday task, it is essential to spend time examining it in detail and working out each little step in the process. Only then can a clear and logical set of instructions be established. These instructions should be written down to ensure consistency when training.

It may seem unnecessary to have to work out and write down instructions for a task you know so well. In fact, this is an essential part of successful Lifeskills teaching. I firmly believe that it is often careless, badly planned teaching, rather than a trainee's limited capacity to learn, that results in a skill not being mastered.

If you can identify this flaw in your own experience of training, or in what you have observed, then you have made a significant step in the right direction. *Task analysis* is the key to developing clear and logical instructions.

TASK ANALYSIS

This is the process of breaking a task down into its simplest elements. Task analysis identifies the simplest sequence of actions which will allow the completion of a task to the required standard. It is an essential stage in the preparation of any Lifeskills training programme.

Task analysis can be a very elaborate, detailed and time-absorbing procedure. In rigorous analysis, endless time can be spent recording, very precisely, the sequence of movements an individual makes to perform a task and the exact time and frequency with which each movement occurs. Automatic recording, such as video film, can be used to increase the accuracy of the analysis. Such procedures will indeed lead to an extremely accurate analysis, but is such scrutiny essential? It is important to be realistic and to find a balance between the available resources (time in particular) and the detail required for this procedure.

Carrying out a task analysis makes the instructor think clearly and logically about what she is about to teach. The following is a simple, effective method for completing a task analysis. There are four steps:

1 Select a task.
2 Define the task to suit the individual.
3 Break down the task into its simplest elements.
4 Draw up a checklist.

Each of these steps will be explained in detail.

1 Select a task

This has been examined in Chapter 3.

2 Define the task to suit the individual

We all have a tendency to talk about tasks in general terms—for example, I am going to teach Nessa how to clean the kitchen after a meal. What does that mean? How clean is clean? One interpretation of 'clean the kitchen after a meal' may be:

Wash the dishes, leave them in the drainer to dry, wipe the worktops and sweep the floor.

Another interpretation of the same task might be:

Wash, dry and put away the dishes, clean the sink and wash the drying cloth. Clear the table and worktops, putting everything away in its proper place. Clean worktops and cupboard doors. Clean the hob of the cooker, removing any spills or marks. Empty the bin, sweep and mop the floor.

It is obvious from this example that a much greater range of skills would be required for the second interpretation.

General, non-specific tasks such as 'clean the kitchen' are sometimes called *fuzzies*. They are open to vague and subjective definition. When doing a task analysis it is important to avoid fuzzies and be very exact.

Here are some examples of fuzzies compared with clearly defined tasks (adapted from *Work Options Training Manual '92*).

Fuzzies	*Clear Definitions*
Improve her self-care.	Wash her own hair on a Saturday.
Develop leisure skills.	Go bowling with a friend once a month.
Learn how to read and write.	Write own name and address legibly without assistance.

Fuzzies often sound impressive and set out to achieve a lot, but they are usually vague and endless, making it difficult to know when they have been achieved. It is then impossible to know when to celebrate!

In order to carry out a clear and time-efficient task analysis, the instructor should know exactly what she is analysing. Just like defining a goal (see Chapter 3), it must be clear:

- What has to be done.
- Under what conditions.
- To what degree of success.

A task can only be defined in this way in relation to a known individual. For example, the *individual task* 'Hair Care' could be accurately defined for two different people in two different ways.

Real Life Examples

Vicky has completed two years of vocational training. She is due to begin a three-month work placement in a restaurant in the near future. The importance of personal appearance has been stressed and, in this regard, Vicky and her instructor agree that something will need to be done with her hair, which is very curly and difficult to manage.

Vicky has always washed her hair herself and her mother trims it for her whenever necessary. It is agreed that Vicky needs to go to a hairdresser to get some advice and have her hair styled. Vicky has not been to a hairdresser before.

For Vicky, 'Hair Care' is defined as follows: Attend a chosen hairdresser independently at agreed regular intervals and budget for so doing.

Alison leads a very sheltered and dependent life. Until recently her mother has carried out all Alison's self-care activities. It is agreed that if Alison is to go on holiday with her club in the summer, which she is very keen to do, her self-care skills will have to improve. Over the past three months she has worked very hard and is now delighted to be able to dress herself with the exception of fastening buttons, belts and laces. She would now like to be able to brush her own hair and keep it tidy with a hairband.

For Alison 'Hair Care' is defined as follows: Every morning, after dressing herself, she will identify her own hairbrush and independently brush her own hair until there are no more knots. She will then put on the chosen hairband.

These two interpretations of 'Hair Care' illustrate how important it is to tailor a task to suit the individual's needs.

In defining a task, *the criterion* is the standard to which the trainee is expected to perform that task. Confusion occurs easily if the criterion is not agreed in advance and stated clearly. For example, if John is to learn how to make a sandwich:

- Is it acceptable for him to get a little help?
- Is one variety of sandwich filling satisfactory?
- How often does he have to put this task into action?
- At what point can you say that John has acquired the skill?

The criterion may refer to all or any of the following:

- accuracy
- frequency
- assistance allowed
- safety
- speed

The criterion should always be within reach and should be decided in accordance with:

- The individual's needs.
- The individual's capability.
- The resources available.

For example, 'Sandwich Making' could be defined clearly for John as: To make two varieties of sandwich without help. John will make his sandwiches for work each evening, alternating the fillings.

3 Break down the task into its simplest elements

In order to break down the task accurately the instructor should:

a Complete the task slowly herself or observe someone competent perform the task (in the situation in which the trainee will do it). It is important that the task should be completed in the appropriate situation in order that the outcome will relate to the individual trainee. For example, if a trainee is to learn how to grill two slices of bacon, there is not much point in analysing this task in the kitchen at work, using an electric cooker, if the trainee has a gas cooker at home.

b Write down every step which is involved in the process and the sequence in which it occurs. For example:

Task—Go to the local cinema with a friend

1 Buy a newspaper.
2 Look up the film guide.
3 Select and agree on a film.
4 Write down or memorise name of film.
5 Check what time film is on.
6 Check the price of a cinema ticket.
7 Plan a time and place at which to meet.
8 Work out what time to leave home.

9 Walk to the bus stop.
10 Travel by bus to meeting place.
11 Meet friend.
12 Walk to cinema.
13 Go to the ticket desk.
14 Queue if necessary.
15 Ask for one ticket for (state name of film).
16 Pay money, wait for change.
17 Take ticket.
18 Go to the cinema shop if necessary!
19 Show ticket to ticket checker.
20 Keep ticket/counterfoil.
21 Show ticket/counterfoil to usher.
22 Sit where indicated by usher.
23 Identify location of ladies/gents toilets.
24 Identify emergency exits.
25 Observe lights going out when film is due to begin.
26 Watch film and, if you need to speak, whisper quietly.
27 If eating, eat quietly.
28 If visiting the toilet, do so quietly.
29 Observe lights coming on again when film is over.
30 Stand up, check you have all your belongings.
31 Leave cinema.
32 Walk to your bus stop and catch the bus home.

(This example is based on prior knowledge of the community, ability to use public transport and literacy and numeracy skills.)

When the task has been broken down into its simplest elements, the instructor should do the task, as though for the first time, following exactly the steps which have been listed. In going through each step of the task analysis with the trainee, the instructor may find that she has broken the task into too many steps—for instance, that two steps in the process cannot easily be separated. On the other hand, she might find that there are gaps where an important aspect of the task was omitted.

This process should show whether or not the instructions are adequate and in the right order. *Make any necessary adjustments to the task analysis.*

4 Draw up a checklist

A checklist is formed from the task analysis. Each step is written as a positive statement in the third person, to which a Yes/No answer can apply. A checklist is used to assess the trainee's ability in relation to a specific task. It is completed with the trainee prior to the training programme and after its completion. As each step is observed it should be marked with a tick if the trainee can do it and a nought if the trainee cannot do it. This sort of checklist is often called a pre- and post-test. By taking the trainee through the listed steps in the appropriate setting, before beginning the training programme (as a pre-test), the instructor can identify what the trainee already knows. This information forms the baseline for the training programme, which always acknowledges the trainee's existing abilities.

When the training programme has been completed, the instructor should go through the checklist step by step while the trainee completes the task (as a post-test), to ensure that every aspect of the task has been mastered and to identify any weak spots which might exist and require further attention.

The checklist for the task 'going to the cinema with a friend' might look like the one on the next page:

Lifeskills

NAME: _____

	Pre-test Date	**Post-test Date**
TASK: Going to the cinema with a friend		
Buys a newspaper		
Looks up the film guide		
Selects and agrees on a film		
Cuts relevant piece out of paper		
Checks what price a ticket is		
Arranges a time and place to meet friend		
Works out what time to leave home		
Travels to town by bus		
Meets friend at the cinema		
Goes to the ticket desk		
Queues if necessary		
Asks for one ticket to see (names film)		
Pays money, waits for change		
Takes ticket, minds it carefully		
Goes to the cinema shop if necessary		
Shows ticket to the ticket collector		
Follows the ticket collector's directions to right cinema		
Shows the ticket to the usher		
Sits where indicated by usher		
Identifies ladies and gents toilets		
Identifies emergency exits		
Knows when film is about to start		
Watches film quietly		
Knows when film is over		
Stands up and checks all belongings		
Leaves cinema through main exits		
Walks to bus stop		
Catches the right bus home		

5 Planning The Training Programme

By this point we have completed the background work, namely becoming familiar with the Lifeskills Network and really getting to know the trainee and his wishes for the future.

We have 'set the scene' for the individual by agreeing long-, medium- and short-term goals, towards which the trainee is motivated to work. We have selected one task to begin with, analysed that task and established what the trainee already knows and, therefore, where training needs to start.

You are now ready to plan the training programme. Careful planning is essential as it will directly affect the success with which the skill is learnt. As I mentioned before, I am convinced that poor teaching, rather than limited capacity to learn, is often responsible for a trainee's lack of progress.

On-the-spot planning of training sessions is very common. This cannot be efficient. It eats into the time that has been made available for training. It stops the flow of the session, causing confusion and loss of concentration. It reduces the sense of importance which trainees feel. This type of training is more about filling time than genuinely passing on skills. Progress is likely to be slow and morale low.

Key point
The importance which the instructor attributes to the training programme plays a large part in motivating the trainee.

Real Life Example

Brian, a workshop supervisor, was planning an eight-week training programme. His aim was to teach four trainees how to go to the shop for some groceries.

Brian had completed the task analysis, drawn up a check list and identified what skills each trainee had previously acquired. He decided that the first training session would concentrate on making a shopping list. Brian had fully intended to plan this session but had been very busy and simply didn't have the time.

At 9 o'clock on the Wednesday morning (the agreed time) Brian's group was waiting for him in the canteen.

Brian: Good morning all.
Trainee: Where are we working, Brian?
Brian: I'm not quite sure. Could you stay in the canteen for a few minutes while I check?

> *First mistake: room not organised.*

Brian went off hoping that Room A would be available. However, there was an activity taking place there, which Brian had not anticipated, and it took him twenty minutes to organise the use of another room. At 9:30 the group members were seated in a very large and quite unsuitable room. Brian apologised, saying that he would make sure they would have the use of Room A for the following week.

Brian: You are all very welcome to this training programme which aims to train you to go shopping for groceries independently. During this programme we shall be going through the whole process of shopping, ensuring that you can manage each step.
                What is the first thing you have to do when you need to go shopping?
Trainee: Put on your coat.
Brian: Yes, but that comes a little later. The first step is to make out a shopping list.
Trainee: What shall we put on the list?

Brian had not thought this out. He had not decided what they were making the list for. He felt quite uneasy but covered up by making a quick decision on the spot.

Brian: We are going to make sandwiches which you can eat at lunch time. What kind of sandwiches would you like to make?

Trainees: Ham/cheese/tuna fish.

> **Second mistake: jumps on to new skill.**

They agreed to make ham and cheese sandwiches.

Brian: If we are going to make ham and cheese sandwiches, what shall we need to buy in the shops?
Trainees: Bread, ham, cheese, butter.

Brian wrote the words up on a chart.

Brian: Could you all write those items down?
Trainees: I have no pen, neither do I. . . .

> **Third mistake: materials not prepared.**

Brian had to go off to get pens and paper. This took ten minutes. Then the trainees began to write. Brian knew that two of the trainees could copy-write but not read what they had written. He had intended to think of some way of getting round this problem, but had not had time. He was annoyed with himself.

Brian: Have you all written down those items?
Trainees: Yes.
Brian: What should we do now?
Trainee: Put on our coats and go to the shops.
Brian: Right, let's do that.

As they were getting ready to go, Brian realised that he did not have enough money and would have to ask the workshop manager for petty cash.

> **Fourth mistake: requirements not anticipated.**

The workshop manager was at a meeting, so he had to borrow money from another member of staff. It was 10:30 before they were ready to leave.

Trainee: What about our tea break? We'll never be back by 10:45.

> **Fifth mistake: no time plan.**

Brian: I never thought of that. Yes, I suppose we should wait
            until after the tea break. We'll take off our coats,
            then, and get out the utensils which we will need later
            for making sandwiches.
Trainee: What is 'utensils'?
Brian: It's the word used for the 'tools' in the kitchen, the
            things you use to prepare and cook food—knives,
            wooden spoons, cheese graters, and so on.

At 11:10 the tea break was over, coats were on again and they
were ready to go. One of the group members was a very slow
walker and it took her half an hour to get to the shop, normally a
ten-minute walk away.

> *Sixth mistake: no anticipation of difficulties.*

Trainee: What type of bread shall we get, Brian?
Brian: A large sliced loaf.
Trainee: How much cheese, Brian?
Brian: I don't know, I suppose two packets of eight slices.

> *Seventh mistake: instructor unsure what he is doing.*

The two group members who could not read were unable to
participate very much: they just watched. As they chose the
foods from the list, Brian talked about how to select food. He
explained how to tell if it was fresh and drew the trainees'
attention to the sell-by dates. However, he gave much too much
information at once and most of it was not taken in. Brian was
confused himself, as he had really intended to include this
information in a later session.

> *Eighth mistake: giving too much information.*

The shopping took half an hour and they arrived back at the
workshop at 12:45, with lunch break fast approaching at 1:00.
Brian had to make the sandwiches quickly himself, in order to
have them ready for 1 o'clock. The group members watched.

Result: Brian felt tired, flustered and dissatisfied. He knew the
session had been a disaster.

The trainees had enjoyed the break from work but they certainly had not learnt anything worthwhile. Unless the instructor has planned in advance exactly what information each training session will cover, he or she is likely to rush ahead, giving too much information. Brian had allowed eight training sessions to cover the skill of going shopping independently. He had intended to limit the first session to teaching the trainees how to make a shopping list. He would ensure, by using a range of teaching methods and examples, that this step was fully understood. Instead, because he was unprepared, he rushed ahead, giving much too much information. In fact he touched on at least seven different steps of the skill in just one training session:

- Making a shopping list.
- Going to the shop.
- Finding the required foods.
- Selecting fresh foods.
- Paying for the goods.
- Putting the goods into bags.
- Using the purchased goods.

Key point
It is very difficult to focus on each aspect of a skill in adequate detail unless you are well prepared.

Endless time could be devoted to planning training sessions meticulously, down to the finest detail. No doubt the resulting training sessions would be very effective. However, as with all aspects of Lifeskills training, the time available must be used to its best advantage. It is essential that some time be given to planning the programme—just enough time to ensure that the instructor (having already selected a skill and completed a task analysis) knows:

- When the training will take place.
- Where the training will take place.
- What exactly each session will cover.
- What materials and resources will be required.
- What teaching methods will be used.
- That each step of the skill has been included.
- That obvious difficulties have been anticipated.

Real life—a better way

Before the course was due to start, Brian took two Wednesday mornings to plan it carefully. Some saw this as a waste of time and thought it would have been more productive to get on with the training programme: 'Brian knows very well how to go shopping. What is he preparing?' However, as was clear in the previous example, poor planning leads to wastage of both instructor's and trainees' time. This time, Brian knew exactly what he was doing:

Session 1	Wednesday, 9.00 a.m.–1.00 p.m.
Location	Room A
Topic	Making a shopping list
Materials needed	Paper, pens, worksheets, some old magazines, glue, some empty product boxes and packets 2 doz. pieces of stiff card 2 plastic wallets.
Teaching methods	Discussion, making choices quiz, helping each other cutting and glueing, role play, writing/worksheets.
Anticipated difficulties	Literacy problems

Brian met the four trainees in Room A at 9.00 a.m. He welcomed them to the training programme, confirmed that they were all keen to take part, and knew exactly what the goal was. He outlined briefly what he hoped they would cover in each session and they agreed to review this plan half-way through.

Having clarified that this, the first training session, was all about making a shopping list, Brian gave out a clear worksheet to each trainee. At the top of the worksheet Brian had drawn a cup of tea and a ham and cheese sandwich. Underneath, there were three instructions:

1 Write down the foods which you need to make a ham and cheese sandwich and a cup of tea.
2 Check in the kitchen to see if you have any of these items already. If so, cross those items out.
3 Write down amounts/number of each item that is needed.

Brian went through the three steps slowly with the group, involving them and their ideas as much as possible. He wrote the details clearly on a large chart. The trainees then filled in the worksheets.

Brian then explained that two members of the group had some difficulty with reading. He said that this was a common difficulty and that there were two simple ways round it:

a They could ask for help from a shop assistant. Brian set up a role-play to practise doing this in an appropriate and adult way.

b   They could use pictures. Brian explained a simple method of making a shopping list with pictures. He gave each trainee twelve blank cards. He asked the trainees who could read to use this skill to help the trainees who had difficulty reading. Being asked to help made them feel important and they did so gladly. Brian pointed out that all trainees had different strengths and weaknesses and that we should all be able to give and accept help. The four trainees had to find and cut out small pictures of common foods from a bundle of old magazines, looking particularly for the items on the shopping list they had just made. They stuck these pictures onto the pieces of card. The two trainees who could not read now had a bank of twenty-four pictures of common foods which they could expand gradually. When going shopping, they could select the pictures of the foods that they needed and put them in a little wallet. In the shop they could then look through the pictures and be reminded of what to buy. They practised this procedure.

Brian then set up a practical shopping exercise. He had collected about twenty empty cartons and packets of common grocery products. He set these out on the table. One by one, he gave each trainee a list of six items to find in the 'shop'. The two non-readers used the picture and wallet system to remember the items which they had to find. The others used written lists. He then swapped the lists round and, to add some fun and motivation, he timed each trainee to see who could find the six items in the shortest time.

Before the session finished, each trainee was given a work-sheet to complete at home and bring in the next week. The worksheet was simple and would remind the trainees what they had learnt in the session. It listed ten food items (with picture symbols) which were required to make a dinner. Then there was a question: 'If you already had (three given items) at home, what would you need to buy, to make the dinner? Make a shopping list in writing or pictures.'

Result of this training session: Brian felt satisfied that he had prepared and run a successful and enjoyable training session.

The group members had had a busy and interesting morning.

Each trainee understood the basic steps in making a shopping list. Those who had difficulty reading were particularly pleased with their new method, and those who could read were proud to have helped them.

There is a world of a difference between the two Real Life examples given. The first was an insult to the trainees and a frustrating waste of time for the instructor; the second, smooth and productive for all concerned. The key factor responsible for the difference was the preparation.

> **Key point**
> *Careful preparation shows respect for the trainee, leads to an efficient training session and yields better results.*

HOW TO PLAN A TRAINING PROGRAMME

Over the ten years during which I have been involved in Life-skills training, I have gradually identified the steps in the process of planning a training programme. With the absence of any guidelines when I set out, I took many wrong roads and made countless mistakes from which I have learnt a great deal. I have been continually refining and improving my approach to planning training programmes incorporating these experiences. I now feel confident that the resulting guidelines will steer the instructor clearly through this process. The steps given aim to provide a basic formula that can be applied to the training of any skill, at any level, with an individual or a group. The eight steps in planning a training programme are:

1 Identify how much time you have to devote to the training programme.
2 Decide who the training programme is for and the skill it will cover.
3 Invite the trainee(s) to take part in the training programme.
4 Liaise with the trainee's family or supervisor.
5 Complete a pre-test with the trainee.
6 Draw up a timetable for the training programme.
7 Anticipate difficulties which may arise.
8 Draw up an agreement with the trainee.

An important thread which must run right through the planning and implementation of a training programme is the recognition that the trainee is an adult and should always be treated as such. The training programme must, therefore, be age-appropriate in every way. The dignity of adults who have learning disabilities tends to be undermined, usually due to habit or lack of thought rather than any bad intention. Nevertheless, the effect is very undesirable. Trainees who are not treated as adults are often dependent and unmotivated, with low self-esteem and few opportunities to make choices. Lifeskills training aims to counteract this by empowering them to be more confident and independent and to strive for a better quality of life. The whole approach to training must therefore practise what it preaches! One clear rule of thumb is to involve the trainee as much as possible in making decisions about the training programme. Encourage him to give opinions and make suggestions and then ensure that he can see his suggestions being used or seriously considered.

Step 1: Identify how much time you have to devote to the training programme

Whether you are a busy parent with other family members to look after, or a worker with responsibility for a large group, you must decide what time you can make available to devote to a particular training programme. If your whole brief is Lifeskills training, you must still allocate specific tme to each programme you undertake. Once this has been established, you will have clear parameters within which to work. *Whatever* time you have to devote to training, no matter how short, is worthwhile. The secret is to be realistic about what you aim to achieve and *not* to take on too much.

It may be necessary to seek permission or inform others of your intention to use the allocated time for Lifeskills training. In a work situation, it could mean taking time out of the normal routine to undertake a training programme, in which case another worker may have to cover for you. In a home situation, it could mean being unavailable to other family members for a short period of time. This should be explained in advance to avoid any misunderstandings.

Time can be allocated in a range of different ways. One instructor may run a training programme for one hour each day over a period of several weeks. Another might devote a whole day per week for a few weeks. A third option would be to work all day every day, for a shorter length of time. The decision depends on:

- What is suitable for the instructor and relevant others.
- What is suitable for the trainee(s).
- What is suitable for that particular skill.

The important factor is not the length of time the trainee takes to learn a particular skill but rather that the time-scale is realistic and that the skill is mastered.

Step 2: Decide who the training programme is for and the skill it will cover

In a work setting, there may be several trainees whose needs are obvious and who have identified dreams and goals for the future. The process of selecting a skill and agreeing a short-term goal will have helped each person to identify a starting point. It is then up to the instructor to prioritise which trainee's needs should be met first. This of course, could depend on several factors—the circumstances in which the trainee lives, the quality of his life, the changes that this skill would bring about, and the opportunities that the trainee has already had.

It is very important that the instructor should make a decision and then stick firmly to it. It is very easy to get lost in a sea of needs where different priorities keep coming to the surface. If the instructor tries to attend to all these needs she may end up tackling none of them properly.

In a situation where a few trainees share the same need or wish to progress in the same direction, it is possible to plan and implement a programme for a group of up to six. Trainees can benefit from learning together and yet be facilitated to progress at their own pace. When planning to work with a group, the instructor should consider whether it is best for group members to be:

a   Mixed male and female
In most cases this is preferable. However, there may be certain skills such as aspects of personal hygiene or sexuality that could

be more successfully or easily managed with a single-sex group.
When the subject matter of a training programme is going to deal
with sensitive sexual or personal issues, it may also be more
appropriate for a female instructor to work with women and a
male to work with men. Even if the instructor feels that he or she
has no inhibitions, it is important to consider the feelings of the
trainee whose life may have been more sheltered, causing him or
her to get embarrassed more easily.

b   Mixed ability
Sometimes it can be an advantage to make up a group with
trainees of mixed ability. Those who are more skilled can be
encouraged to help out those who are less skilled, and this can be
of mutual benefit. Those helping out often feel important and
satisfied with their contribution, and those of lower ability may
be better motivated and more determined when learning from
their peers.

It is not always possible to include trainees with a range of
abilities in one group. This depends largely on the subject matter
of the training programme. For example, in literacy and numeracy training, if the trainees' ability levels vary considerably
within a group, there will be little or no option for group work or
group instruction. In that case the instructor is working with each
trainee individually, and the preparation and implementation of
the training session can be time-consuming and frustrating.
While group training programmes should always facilitate each
trainee in progressing at his own pace, some subjects lend
themselves much more easily to being taught within a mixed
ability group.

c   Mixed ages
For most Lifeskills training programmes age would not be an
important issue. There are, however, some situations that may
run more smoothly with trainees of similar ages, so this is worth
bearing in mind. For example, with a group learning community
skills, when selecting activities which group members would
enjoy together, remember that younger people would probably
be attracted to different activities from older people.

d   Mixed personalities

In any group there will automatically be a mix of personalities and this of course is desirable. It is important, however, to use your knowledge of the individuals to avoid personality clashes or including people who do not get along together. While it would be a general aim of Lifeskills training that people should be tolerant of each other and try to get along, the instructor must guard against unnecessary time wastage and disruption. For example, in a communication skills group, if two of the group members have a history of not getting on together, a situation may arise when one will say, 'I'm not going to talk about anything private if *he's* here,' or in a community skills group, 'Well, I'm not going out if she's coming.' This sort of scenario can be very disruptive and upsetting and have a very negative effect on the learning process for the whole group. Special training programmes can be established to deal with this sort of problem, but this should be done separately for the trainees in question.

It is important to acknowledge that many people who work with adults who have learning disabilities do not have the option of 'selecting' a group to work with. Very often they are allocated a particular group of trainees, maybe as many as 15 or 20, for whom they have total responsibility. Obviously, this makes Lifeskills training more difficult. One well-tried approach to dealing with this situation is known as Room Management (Porterfield and Blunden, 1978). This aims to combine interesting and useful activities for a group of people, with structured teaching sessions for individuals or small groups amongst them. A minimum of two staff members is required. One takes the role of room manager or overall supervisor. He or she may supervise the regular work activity or may set up a general group activity in which everyone can participate, such as art, keep fit or a quiz. The second staff member can carry out a structured Lifeskills training programme with a selected individual or small group. The roles may then be reversed, so that each staff member is afforded the opportunity to work with the large and the small group. Some agencies with large groups of trainees have a 'floating' member of staff to facilitate this sort of arrangement.

For parents, 'deciding who the training programme is for' is hardly a relevant topic as, obviously, their whole focus is on their own son or daughter. However, I have encountered parents whose sons or daughters have a common problem or share a particular goal and who, by linking up and working together, achieve great results. This sort of arrangement gives great support to the parents and often added enjoyment and motivation to the trainees.

Real Life Example

Brenda and Marian lived in the same area. Each lived at home with one parent. In the future Brenda hoped to live independently and Marian planned to live with her sister. Both women needed to become actively involved in the running of the home but seemed to have very little motivation to do so. As far as they were concerned, independent living was a thing of the future. At present each had her mother to do things for her. The mothers met each other by chance at a meeting in the workshop where their daughters worked. They identified the similarities in their situations and decided to meet up and see if they could work together on this.

They began by training their daughters in how to prepare an evening meal. Each learned in her own home and worked towards inviting the other over for an independently prepared meal. Then they set up a weekly meeting at which a small goal for the following week was agreed. At the meeting the mothers and daughters reported on progress and discussed difficulties that had arisen. With the added motivation, interest and competition, both women made great progress in developing home skills. They also developed a lasting friendship.

Step 3: Invite the trainee to take part in the training programme

Keeping in mind an age-appropriate and respectful approach, the instructor should explain carefully to the trainee that he is being offered an opportunity to avail himself of some training. Once the trainee understands what he is being offered, when and where it will take place, he must be given a genuine choice regarding acceptance or non-acceptance of the offer.

In many cases a training programme is carefully planned with a trainee's greatest needs and wishes in focus. When it comes to the stage of informing the trainee, much of the benefit can be lost by the manner in which the trainee is told of this opportunity.

Real Life Example

Supervisor:	Martin, could you come here, please. I have something to tell you.
Martin:	Am I in trouble?
Supervisor:	No, you're not in trouble. You are starting a training programme next week. I have organised with the boss to have time on Tuesday mornings to work with you on numeracy skills.
Martin:	What's that?
Supervisor:	It's all to do with numbers and counting.
Martin:	But I already know how to count.
Supervisor:	Ah, but there is much that you don't know. Do you remember when we were discussing your future, where you might go and what you might do? You mentioned that you don't understand how to use money properly.
Martin:	Oh yeah. Will I be learning that?
Supervisor:	Well, you just wait and see. We will work in the small office at 11 o'clock each Tuesday for eight weeks. All right?
Martin:	Eh—well—I suppose so. Do I have to ask the boss?
Supervisor:	No, it's all sorted out.

Not only does an approach like this actively undermine the trainee, it also wastes a perfect opportunity to develop the trainee's personal identity, acknowledge his strengths, increase motivation, involve him in decision-making, offer him choices and show him genuine respect.

Key point
If the procedure of inviting a trainee to take part in a training programme is handled carefully, then the

*trainee benefits and his confidence increases even before
the training begins.*

When inviting a trainee to take part in a training programme, the
instructor should:

a   Invite the trainee(s) to a meeting at a mutually suitable time
The purpose of this meeting is to inform the trainee(s) of the
instructor's intention to run a training programme and discuss all
the details in relation to it. Even if the training programme is
being organised in the less formal setting of the home, the parent
should agree a particular time to sit down with her son or
daughter to discuss the plans. An organised meeting at an agreed
time, no matter how short, immediately gives the impression
that something important is about to happen.

*b   Clarify why this trainee was selected and what skill the
     training programme will deal with*
The best explanation the instructor can give to a trainee is that he
requested this opportunity himself. So the instructor might say,
'When we were completing your personal profile, you said . . .'
or 'At your last individual programme planning meeting, you
suggested . . .' or 'When we were discussing your future plans
with the family recently, you asked . . .' If the training programme being offered to the trainee really relates to something
that he has requested, this should be acknowledged to the full. It
puts the trainee in the strong position of being the master of his
destiny. That is a very desirable position and one that gives the
trainee great motivation to learn. Even in a situation where some
mundane skills have to be learnt before the *real* goal comes into
sight, ALWAYS refer back to the trainee's own wishes:
    'When we discussed your future some weeks ago, you said that
most of all, you would like a job minding children. One very
important skill in minding children is to have good control over
your own temper. You told me that you sometimes have a
problem with losing your temper and that this has got you into
trouble in the past. Would you like to take part in a training
programme which is designed to help you control your temper . . . ?'
    In some cases, trainees are referred for training programmes

for needs identified by others—for example, a personal hygiene problem that cannot be tolerated in the work-room, or for independent travel training because funding for special transport has been reduced. In situations such as these, it is up to the instructor to make these skills meaningful to the trainee in terms of his wishes for the future. For example:

'Michael, you told me some time ago that you are very keen to do a night class in woodwork. I would be very happy to investigate that possibility with you. However, I must be honest with you and say that we have an important matter to sort out first. That is, your personal hygiene . . .'

c   Outline what the training programme aims to cover
Make it clear to the trainee exactly what he will be learning during the training programme, and what the programme aims to achieve. Ask him what he thinks of the content. Is there anything that should be included or taken out? Explain the methods of training that will be used and how these will help him to learn.

For example, in the training programme for 'going to the shop for groceries' which was discussed at the start of this chapter, the instructor might explain:

During this training programme, four trainees will work together learning all the skills of shopping. We will cover how to make a list, finding your way to the shop, getting to know the shop, finding what you want, paying the money, packing your goods, and so on.
   To learn each of these new skills, we will work in many different ways:
We will plan to cook a lunch and decide what ingredients we need to buy for it.
We will make up our own shop and use it for practice.
We will role-play, acting out what you should say in the shop.
We will talk about money and change and how best to cope with it.
We will all go to the shop together, putting the skills into practice.
I will go with each of you separately to your own local shop, so that you are familiar with it and confident to shop there.

Key point
Only when you give the trainee adequate information is he in a position to make a decision as to whether or not he wishes to take part.

When explaining what the training programme will involve, every effort should be made to make it sound interesting and inviting. With the more mundane skills that have to be mastered in order to reach a desired goal, enticement may be required to boost interest. For example: 'When we go shopping together we must visit the new coffee shop and have a cuppa and a good chat . . .'

d Explain when and where the training programme should take place
By the time this meeting takes place, the instructor will have checked out her own available time. However, there may still be some flexibility on how this time is used or allocated. The instructor may say, for example, 'I will be running this programme one morning a week for ten weeks. When you decide whether or not you will join the programme, we can decide which morning is most suitable.'

She should also indicate where she intends to run the course, detailing use of community facilities and so on, where relevant. Where there is scope for involving trainees in this decision, the final arrangements can be made with those who choose to take part in the programme.

e Detail any special requirements for the training programme
It is important for the trainee(s) to be aware of any factor that might affect his decision to take part in the programme.

Will he require money, materials, permission from home or work, time off, particular support or assistance, time to complete work at home, and so on?

So long as the trainee knows any requirements in advance, he will be able to consider these and avoid the embarrassment of having something sprung on him during the programme, that poses a problem.

f Give the trainee(s) plenty of time to ask questions, give opinions and share ideas
Having left most aspects of the training programme plan open-ended, there is room to include the trainee's suggestions. The

instructor should be sure to allow adequate time during or at the end of the meeting for the trainee to gather and express his ideas and reactions. Some trainees will have to be encouraged and prompted to give a response. Others may want to alter the entire plan and create something different. The instructor should aim to find a balance between facilitating changes and ensuring that they are reasonable and justifiable.

She should listen to and accept all opinions given by the trainees in order to create a positive atmosphere. The trainee is then likely to feel more confident and respected and, as a result, will benefit more from the training programme.

g   Give the trainee a genuine choice

After the trainee has been given all the relevant information and has had the opportunity to ask questions and contribute ideas, he should be asked to go off and think about the option for a while, allowing him time to discuss it with whoever he chooses.

A time should be set for him to come back with his mind made up. It should be made clear that it is the trainee's choice and that the instructor will not be annoyed or insulted if he turns down the opportunity. Too often, trainees feel under pressure to say what they think others want to hear. This is simply a lack of confidence that an appropriate approach to training will help to overcome. The process of 'inviting a trainee to take part in the training programme' may seem unnecessary and time-consuming. In fact, it is essential and can be completed in an hour or less. Once the instructor has her information together and knows exactly what she is offering, the meeting should run smoothly.

If an instructor is going to devote her time to this training programme over the next 10 to 12 weeks or more, *that* one hour is a small investment to make in order to ensure that the participants are interested and well motivated. If a trainee ultimately decides not to be involved, despite all encouragement, the instructor should not feel that she has wasted a lot of time discussing and outlining the programme. Instead she should focus on the fact that many hours have not been wasted working with a trainee who is an unmotivated or reluctant participant.

Key point
Time spent clarifying exactly what is on offer and what

the programme hopes to achieve helps to avoid the situa-
tion of training people who don't want to be trained.

Regardless of the level of ability of the trainee, the instructor should make every effort to facilitate him in understanding what is being offered to him and allow him a genuine choice.

Step 4: Liaise with the trainee's family or supervisor

Liaison with the trainee's family does not suggest that the trainee cannot make a decision or speak up for himself. On the contrary, one of the main aims of Lifeskills training is to encourage the trainee to take more responsibility for himself and his future. Appropriate contact with families or supervisors can aid this process by giving the instructor additional information and by reinforcing the learning that takes place. It is important to remember that our aim is for the trainee to master a new skill that will bring him closer to where or what he wants to be. Any assistance in this must be welcomed. It is not *always* necessary to inform parents or supervisor. This depends largely on the individual trainee, his lifestyle and the particular skill being taught. The instructor should decide the merits of gaining the support of others, and if she considers it beneficial, she should seek the trainee's approval before contacting others.

In my own experience, endless time has been saved by talking to those who are close to the trainee. In relation to particular skills, they can often give valuable information that helps to overcome difficulties and speed the training process. During training they can provide encouragement and show interest in new developments, which are always beneficial. Once the skill has been acquired, they can help to ensure that it is used and maintained and that the trainee's effort is acknowledged and praised.

Real Life Example

Terence was always late for work in the morning. No matter what bonuses were offered or what disciplinary measures were taken, he was always at least twenty minutes late. His aim was to get a job in open employment, and with his ability to drive and operate a fork-lift truck, he had a good chance of realising his dream.

However the question of his punctuality had to be dealt with first. Terence's supervisor at the workshop was keen to help him sort out this problem, and Terence himself could see how important it was if he wanted to get a job. Both were committed to a training programme in punctuality. Sensibly, the supervisor decided that it was important to contact Terence's home to see if anything there was contributing to his repeatedly late arrivals. Reluctantly, Terence agreed to the supervisor contacting his mother. This contact, revealing information about which the supervisor was completely unaware, put a very different slant on the training programme.

Terence had a bed-wetting problem, which he had had all his life. Since becoming an adult, this was more of an embarrassment to him. He did not want his elderly mother to have to change his bed and wash his sheets. So, every morning he removed the sheets from his bed and brought them and his pyjamas to the local launderette. The launderette did not open until nine o'clock—the very time he was due in work. As a result he never got to work until twenty past nine.

Naturally, the time-keeping training programme was now irrelevant and the instructor set out to seek advice and specialist help in dealing with the bed-wetting problem or—second best—teaching Terence to use a washing machine.

When liaising with parents, family or supervisors the instructor should:

- Have the trainee's approval for doing so.
- Inform them briefly of the training programme and what it hopes to achieve.
- Ask their opinion and advice and check for any important relevant information.
- Confirm that if the new skill is acquired, the trainee will be facilitated in using it.
- Check the availability of any necessary resources, such as money for community skills, ingredients for cooking, and so on.

- Encourage them to show interest in what the trainee is doing, to acknowledge achievements and praise generously.
- Facilitate them in contacting her if they make any particular observations.
- *Where necessary*, seek their permission. For example, if training in use of public transport, it would be important to have parental permission in the event of an accident.

One of the greatest resources that can assist trainees in learning new skills is the help and interest of other people. The instructor should make maximum use of this resource, for if she works in isolation, the time and effort that she puts into the training programme may not achieve as much as it should.

Real Life Example

Sarah is 23. She works in sheltered employment four days a week and has a job in a video library for the other day. She is a quiet, hard-working girl. She has suffered from asthma since childhood and as a result has missed a lot of her schooling. Until recently, Sarah could not count and her mother was very concerned about this. She approached various people about her daughter's problem but got no satisfaction. To her great annoyance, it was even suggested that Sarah was too old to learn this skill now.

Sarah's parents worked hard to set up a training pro-gramme at home. They made out number cards, bought number games and devised interesting counting activities. They set goals with Sarah and gave her great support and encouragement. After two months, doing an hour's work two nights a week, Sarah could count up to twenty and knew all the numbers. Her family was delighted and Sarah herself was very pleased.

A month elapsed and then one day, when Sarah was setting six places for dinner, her mother noticed that she was unable to count out six knives and six forks—the skill had faded. Her parents worked on a revision course and it did not take long to brush up on the skill. This time, Sarah's mother contacted her supervisor at work to see if there were any opportunities for Sarah to use her counting skills at work. The supervisor said that she had no idea that Sarah had acquired this skill and that there was plenty of opportunity to use it. In fact, dependable counting ability enabled workers to do quality control—a job that had great status. From then on, Sarah used her counting skills each day, developed them further and never looked back.

Key point
Securing the support and interest of other key people in the training programme can help to bring about better and longer-lasting results.

Step 5: Complete a pre-test with the trainee

A pre-test is a test completed with the trainee prior to the training programme. It establishes, in relation to the selected skill, what the trainee already knows and what he still has to learn. This is an essential step in the process of planning a training programme. The instructor must be aware of the individual's ability and needs if she is planning a programme to meet these needs.

Instructors often make assumptions or generalise about trainees' abilities and needs. This can be insulting, cause a lot of time-wastage and result in missed opportunities to give credit for skills already acquired.

Real Life Example

Let's return to the example of going to the local shop to buy some groceries.

The instructor knew that the four selected trainees could not complete this task independently. He wrongly presumed that they were all at the same level, unable to do *any* part of the task. He analysed the task (see Chapter 4), breaking it down into its simplest parts. The first step was 'Identify what is needed at the shop'. On the first day of the training programme he began to explain this step, using a range of teaching methods. In the course of the training session, he realised that one of the women was already well able to do this and actually had an easier method than the one that he was outlining.

Later in the programme, he spent some time explaining

how each trainee should locate his or her local shop. He had taken the trouble to draw a simple map of each local area, detailing the roads and crossings involved in getting to the shop. In fact, each of the four trainees knew perfectly well how to get to his or her own local shop.

This instructor missed opportunities, therefore, to give trainees credit for the knowledge that they already had. He did not understand that, although they shared the need for the skill of shopping, they were still individuals with a range of abilities in relation to it. He wasted time teaching aspects of the skill that some already knew, and missed the opportunity of giving particular trainees the spotlight to share their experiences and tips with the others.

The pre-test is drawn up directly from the task analysis. It is the checklist that was explained in Chapter 4 (page 75). The instructor should go through each stage of the checklist with the trainee, observing and documenting what he can already do before drawing up the timetable or beginning the training programme. This is why it is called a 'pre'-test. She can then start the training where it is needed and not at some arbitrary point that she has decided. The same test is completed at the end of the training programme. This is called a 'post'-test and it identifies the progress that has been made as a result of the training programme.

The result of the pre-test will direct the instructor in making out the timetable for the training programme. This information is particularly important when working with a group—for example, there may be one member of the group who does not understand a particular stage of the skill with which the others are familiar. In this case the instructor may decide to give that trainee some individual instruction while the others complete a relevant worksheet. Individual differences are much more easily dealt with if they are known in advance.

On the following page is an example of a checklist for the skill of 'going to the local shop to buy some groceries'. It was drawn up by the instructor after completing a task analysis (see Chapter 4, page 73). It was completed with each trainee as a pre-test before the training programme began and helped to shape the way in which the timetable was planned.

CHECKLIST		

Skill: Going to the local shop to buy some groceries
Name: Ann

	Pre-Test	Post-Test
Can identify what goods are needed	✓	
Can write a list (or use symbols)	0	
Can indicate the quantity of each item	0	
Can work out the approximate overall cost	0	
Can carry money safely	✓	
Can put on suitable coat	✓	
Can avoid rain or bring umbrella	✓	
Remembers to bring list	0	
Can find the way to the shops	✓	
Can identify the required shop	✓	
Is familiar with someone helpful in the shop	✓	
Understands the layout of the shop—fresh/ frozen foods, bakery, etc	0	
Can get a trolley/basket	✓	
Can go round the shop in a logical way	0	
Can tell when food is fresh (bread, veg, etc.)	0	
Understands the sell-by dates	0	
Can compare prices where necessary	0	
Can check list with items in basket	0	
Can go to the check-out	✓	
Can behave appropriately with shop staff	✓	
Can ask for help if necessary	✓	
Can put items into bags carefully	0	
Can keep cleaning products separate	0	
Can pay the required money	✓	
Can take receipt and calculate change	0	
Can put money away safely	✓	
Can bring shopping straight home	✓	
Can put items away in their proper places	0	
Test(s) completed	15/1/94	

Step 6: Draw up a timetable for the training programme

This is the central step in the planning of a training programme.
Time invested in drawing up a comprehensive timetable is time
well spent. It is the main reference point throughout the programme and acts as a guide for both instructor and trainee. It
facilitates good planning and preparation of sessions and is one
of the main factors contributing to the efficiency with which goals
are reached. A well-planned timetable allows an instructor to
relax, knowing that no matter how busy she is with other things,
when it comes to the time allocated for training, everything is
ready. The session has been planned, materials organised,
rooms booked, permission sought. There is a great feeling of
comfort and confidence when any undertaking is well organised
and runs smoothly.

Drawing up and following a timetable is another way for the
instructor to show the trainee that the training programme is
important and that his needs and wishes are being taken seriously. Is it fair to expect a trainee, who takes part in a training
session that is planned on the spot, to make any great effort to
improve? It is up to the instructor to set the stage, and in my
experience the trainee's response will rise to the standard that
has been set.

So far in the planning process, the instructor has:

* Identified how much time she can devote to training.
* Having discussed individual needs and plans for the future
  through personal profiles and individual planning meetings,
  has decided which trainee(s) she will work with.
* Invited the trainee(s) to take part in a training programme,
  agreed with them exactly which skill the training programme
  will cover and the times and dates on which it will take place.
* Liaised with trainee's family or supervisor and acquired any
  important additional information as well as their support.
* Drawn up a contract with the trainee (see page 121).
* Completed a task analysis on the agreed skill.
* Completed a pre-test with the trainee(s) to establish what he
  already knows in relation to that skill.

She now has all the necessary information to draw up the
timetable.

A timetable is drawn up directly from the task analysis with the completed pre-test indicating where the training should begin. The task analysis is carefully examined and the instructor decides how best she can convey each required aspect of the skill. Each step being taught and the method of training being used is detailed on the timetable, with the appropriate amount of time allocated to it.

As mentioned before, when defining a task (Chapter 4), statements should be clear and 'fuzzies' should be avoided. The same applies to timetables in order to avoid any uncertainty as to what exactly is being taught on a particular day. A good time-table should indicate clearly:

- What aspect of the skill will be covered in each training session.
- How it will be taught, i.e. what teaching methods and materials will be used.
- When the training session will take place.
- Where the training session will take place.

Making out a timetable is in itself a skill that improves with practice. Instructors have often asked me, 'How do you know how long each step will take?' No one can know this in advance, but with a good knowledge of the trainee and having completed a specific task analysis, the instructor is well equipped to estimate how much time to devote to each step. Flexibility can be built into a timetable to allow for skills being mastered more quickly or slowly than expected—for example, a few relevant work-sheets can be prepared and kept in a file so that, if a training session finishes earlier than expected, trainees are not left twiddling their thumbs. If, on the other hand, some aspect of the skill takes much longer than expected to complete, the timetable may have to be extended or the goal adjusted accordingly. This will be explained in more detail later in this chapter.

> **Key point**
> *Preparing a timetable is the allocating of specific and adequate time to each step of the task analysis and stating how that step will be taught.*

How to draw up a timetable

1　Examine each stage of the task analysis carefully

Unless you have confirmed, by means of the pre-test, that certain elements of the skill have already been mastered, then each one must be covered in the timetable. Some elements will be quick and easy to teach and one training session may incorporate a few. Others may be more complicated and require to be spread over a number of training sessions. Identify which element of the skill is being covered in each training session and decide the most appropriate method of teaching.

2　Each step should be taught in the logical sequence in which it occurs in the task analysis

The sequence in which the skill is taught may affect the speed and efficiency with which it is learnt. For example, if an instructor is teaching a trainee how to make a sandwich, it would not be logical to explain how to put the filling in the sandwich before teaching the trainee how to butter the bread!

3　Each training session should have its own mini-goal

To maximise the satisfaction felt by both trainee and instructor, each training session should aim to achieve something definite. To return to the previous example of making a sandwich: if one training session simply aims to teach the trainee how to butter bread, the instructor should clarify this, with the trainee acknowledging the importance of that step. 'I'd like you to work really hard this morning learning how to butter bread properly. By lunch-time I hope you'll be able to butter a slice of bread without any help. Then we'll both have done a good morning's work.'

4　Make the training sessions as interesting and varied as possible

Training sessions need to be lively and enjoyable in order to hold the trainee's interest and make maximum use of his concentration span. Information can filter through to the trainee in a range of different ways, and the more creative the instructor can be, the better. In order to achieve this, she should avail herself of as many different teaching methods as possible (see Chapter 7).

Similarly, she should make use of a wide range of teaching materials, which can introduce variety as well as making the training process easier. Unfortunately there are not many teaching materials available that are suitable for Lifeskills training with adults. However, the instructor should be aware of what *is* available and use what she can to add interest to the training course.

5 Introduce 'carrots' to boost motivation

Particularly in the more mundane aspects of Lifeskills, motivation can very easily flag and trainee interest wane. A 'carrot' or treat, looming in the near distance, can be a great motivation booster. For example, if a trainee is learning how to look after his own clothes, at a particular point in the timetable he might be invited to dress smartly in the newly laundered or repaired clothes and go out to lunch with the instructor.

6 Allow sufficient time to complete the planned activity

Some skills require a specific amount of time to complete and cannot be broken up or continued at the next session. It is important that the timetable should be realistic in its allocation of time, otherwise training will be rushed and trainees and instructors will be late for other commitments.

For example, if an instructor is training a group of trainees to prepare a meal, she will have to allocate adequate time to allow for the preparing, cooking, eating and clearing up. Therefore one morning a week would be much more suitable for this training programme than one hour each day. Similarly, with a group that is learning some aspect of community skills, time would have to be allowed for travel to and from that community, as well as the time spent there practising the skill.

If the required time is not available, then the instructor should consider whether or not it is advisable to attempt to teach this skill.

7 Include a little time at the start of each training session to recap on what has been learnt already

Because of the time lapse between training sessions, it is very important to recap on what was covered in previous sessions. This process acts as a good introduction to a training session and tunes the trainees' minds back to the task in hand. If the instructor is teaching the skill in its logical sequence, she will automatically include each stage that has been completed when progressing to a new stage. Recapping also provides an opportunity to acknowledge and praise what has been achieved to date.

8 *Where possible, the skill should be taught at the appropriate time of day*

With many skills, the time when they are carried out is not important. Certain skills, however, take place only at particular times of the day, and this should be considered when drawing up a timetable. It is more appropriate to train these skills at the time when they naturally occur. For example, if training a trainee to make a sandwich, it is logical to allocate time for training sessions before lunch so that the prepared sandwich can be eaten at lunch-time. Similarly, if a trainee is learning to dress himself independently, the training should take place when he gets up in the morning, or perhaps after a shower or a swimming class. A skill that is taught out of context is likely to take longer to acquire.

9 *Agree times with the trainee and others*

The instructor should discuss the options regarding time allocation with the trainee(s) and agree a mutually suitable time. Simply to inform a trainee that the training programme is taking place on such a day, at such a time, shows little respect. It assumes that the instructor's time is more valuable than the trainee's and that the trainee has no other commitments. Times can be discussed with the trainee when he is being invited to take part in the training programme. It is also important to consult other relevant people—the manager or members of staff at work and perhaps other family members at home—to ensure that the selected time does not clash with any other plans. Times of training programmes, particularly in a work setting, should be clearly displayed so as to avoid any confusion. If an instructor is running a range of training programmes during the week, a clear weekly timetable stating when and where the training programmes take place, and who is involved, may be necessary. The times of all training sessions should be agreed and approved before making out the timetable. It can be difficult to organise the timing for *all* the required sessions and activities and is therefore very frustrating if major changes have to be made when the timetable has been completed.

10 Check out the location

Decide on the most appropriate location in which to carry out the training programme. Depending on its requirements, certain aspects of the skill may need to be taught at a particular location. Firstly, the instructor should consider all the options, and there may not be many! Try to be as open-minded as possible in considering the range of likely locations. There may be resources in your community that you have not considered. For example, one trainee's brother wanted to set aside some time to help the trainee improve his writing skills. He outlined a plan and together with his brother (the trainee) they agreed a goal. For several nights they worked in the sitting-room on this project, but with the television on and people coming in and out, it was difficult to concentrate. They lost interest and abandoned the project.

Some time later the brother was in the local library, just ten minutes' walk from their home. He noticed a study area that would have been ideal for their literacy project, quiet and comfortable and a recognised place for learning. Following discussions they decided to have another go in the new location. The difference was amazing. The atmosphere in the library was very conducive to learning and the trainee made great progress.

Where possible a skill should be taught in the location in which it occurs. For example, if teaching a trainee how to cross the road safely, some preparatory instruction can be given at home or at work. However, the main instruction should take place in the real situation—at the crossing(s) that the trainee will use most frequently. This is not always practical or easy to organise, but it is worth making the effort if at all possible, as it will be easier for the trainee to put the skill to immediate use. If training in the desired location cannot be arranged, the one used should relate to it as closely as possible and the trainee should subsequently be helped to transfer the skill to his own environment.

It is not simply a matter of suiting the location to the skill; it should also be related to the particular individual. If an instructor is teaching a trainee how to go to the shop for some groceries, there is not much point in the trainee learning all the details of the shop next door to his workshop. It is the shop closest to his home that he needs to go to, so at least some of the training should take place in that shop.

Similarly if a trainee is to improve his personal hygiene, there is no point in training him step by step how to take a shower if he only has a bath at home. It is very important to find out what facilities the trainee has at home, in the workplace and in his community, which relate to the skill he is about to learn. In this way, the instructor can ensure that the training programme is as practical and realistic as it can be, making the best use of all available facilities.

The location of a training programme should enhance the programme where possible. If there is a choice of venues, the instructor should consider the following:

LIGHT. Make sure that there is adequate light to carry out the required activity.

HEAT. Ensure that the room is neither too hot nor too cold to facilitate concentration.

SPACE. Have enough space to carry out the agreed activity comfortably. Some activities will require much more space than others—for example, a group role-play requires much more room than a table activity.

SEATING. Provide adequate room at the table(s) for table-top activities. The chairs should be at an appropriate height. For informal discussion-type sessions where it is important that trainees feel relaxed and at ease, the layout of the room and seating arrangements should be considered.

NOISE. Where possible, choose a quiet location. Noise can interfere with concentration and generally cause distraction.

EQUIPMENT. Ensure that the chosen location provides the necessary equipment and facilities. For example, if the training programme is concentrating on cookery skills, it must be located in a room that has basic kitchen facilities. Similarly, if you are planning to use video or other equipment, the chosen room should have adequate electric sockets and a suitable area to locate the equipment.

Investigate integrated locations for training

With an understanding of the desire of most trainees to integate with other adults, it is important to consider the suitability of integrated locations for training programmes. Where do adults usually learn new skills?

- At adult education classes.
- In third level colleges.
- In literacy schemes.
- In community projects.

Explore these possibilities:

a There may be existing classes that some of your trainees could attend. These will only be beneficial if class material and presentations are pitched at an appropriate level for the trainee to understand.
b Facilities may be made available for the instructor to run her own class in one of these locations.
c Adult education teachers may be prepared to adapt some of their course material in order to run a class at the appropriate level for adults who have learning disabilities but for some reason cannot integrate into an existing class.

In any of these cases, the trainee benefits not only from the content of the training programme but also from integrating with other adults, using college facilities and getting to and from the college.

Real Life Example

An instructor worked with a group of six trainees one afternoon a week for two months, teaching them how to tell the time. They worked in a quiet room inside the workshop. The trainees were interested in the training programme and some progress was made. Because of the nature of the skill the course content was quite monotonous and the instructor observed the trainees' concentration and motivation reducing over time. She investigated some alternative locations in which to run the programme. A local third level college, which ran a day-time programme of adult classes, offered her the use of a room and general facilities such as coffee shop, toilets, photocopiers and so on. The group members were delighted with the suggested change of location and there was a noticeable increase in the rate of progress. The material was the same, the group was the same and the instructor was the same, but the new location had boosted motivation and interest.

The advantages of training programmes being integrated into colleges are:

- It provides a break from the home/work environment.
- It gives the trainee a greater sense of self-importance.
- Trainees observe how others behave in a college environment and learn from this.
- The new environment stimulates interest and boosts motivation.
- Sometimes trainees think learning is only for 'kids at school'. Seeing other adults going to classes can change their minds.
- New situations necessitate decision-making and provide learning opportunities.
- If it is necessary to use public transport, independent travel skills may improve.
- It gives trainees practice in using many public facilities— coffee shop, lifts, toilets, telephones, and so on.
- New friends are often made.
- The general public are called upon to be understanding and facilitating.

For these reasons it is very worthwhile to explore existing adult education facilities in your area. In most countries, adult education authorities promote learning throughout life, for all adults, and those who have learning disabilities must be accommodated in this provision. If you are not satisfied with what is available, perhaps some lobbying for better facilities will be necessary. The 1993 European Commission Green Paper on social policy has a clause that states:

> Social exclusion does not only occur where there is insufficient income. It is manifest in fields such as housing, education, health and access to services. It affects not only individuals, but social groups who are subject to discrimination and segregation. A policy of inclusion must be adopted

to enable and facilitate all individuals to perform a useful role in society.

Having decided on the most suitable location, the instructor should make sure that it will be available at the required times. She may also have to seek permission or approval from somebody in authority, to use the chosen location. If necessary this should be done before the final timetable is drawn up, in order to avoid making changes at a later date.

11   Write the timetable out clearly

Having completed all the preparatory work and considered all the relevant factors, the instructor is now ready to write out the timetable. Since this serves as a guide for instructor and trainees throughout the programme, it must be clear and easy to follow, allowing both parties to see what has been covered and what is coming next. As previously mentioned, it should state what skill the training programme is designed to teach and should give the following information for *each* training session:

- The date of the session.
- The time of the session.
- The location of the session.
- Which element of the skill that session will cover.
- The method of teaching to be used.

Only concise information can be fitted on a timetable. The instructor may, however, require more detailed notes on how the session will be carried out, for example:

The breakdown of the session.
The equipment and materials required.
Notes on individual trainees.
Any preparation needed in advance.

SAMPLE TIMETABLE

The timetable on pages 113–15 shows the programme for teaching the skill 'Going to the local shop to buy groceries', which we have used as an example throughout this chapter. It is based on the task analysis given below.

Task analysis

Identify what is needed.
Write a list.
Work out the quantity of each item.
Work out the overall cost.
Carry money carefully.
Consider weather conditions.
Put on suitable outer clothes.
Find the way to the shop.
Locate the shop itself.
Select a trolley or basket.
Link up with a helpful shop assistant.
Become familiar with shop layout.
Identify different departments: fresh foods, frozen foods, bakery, etc.

Go round the shop in a logical way.
Select required items—prices/freshness/sell-by date.
Place items carefully in basket or trolley.
Check the list with items in basket.
Find the check-out.
Become familiar with procedure at check-out.
Pack items in bags/boxes.
Pay for items.
Take receipt.
Calculate change.
Bring shopping straight home.
Put items away in proper places.

	Wednesday 9 a.m.–1 p.m.	Friday 9 a.m.–1 p.m.
	TIMETABLE FOR 8-WEEK TRAINING PROGRAMME **SKILL—GOING TO THE LOCAL SHOP FOR GROCERIES** Group Members—Freda, Debbie, Paul and Jack	
Wk 1	• Welcome group, recap on course aims, look over 8-week timetable. • Identify basic household products most often needed at the shop. Ask trainees for ideas, record these on flip chart. • Fill in work sheet on 'What might you need if . . .' which shows how to plan ahead.	• Recap—Household Products • Give basic instructions for writing list. • Make a note when things run out • Check cupboards, plan ahead ⎫ Work- • List items— ⎬ sheets. indicate quantities ⎭ • Work out what is needed to make a cup of tea and a ham sandwich, write a list. • A picture method for those who cannot write.
Wk 2	• Discuss prices, are food and household products expensive? Seek trainee opinions. • Divide a given range of products into price brackets: under 50p, under £1, under £2, under £5. • Play 'find the product' game, 20 regular products on the table, each trainee has a list of 5 items. • Find the product and record the price.	• Recap—making a list, guessing the prices. • Go shopping for the tea and sandwich list already prepared. • Discuss appropriate coat/rain gear. • Bring list. • Carry money safely. • Instructor demonstrates shopping procedure. • Return to workshop, make the sandwich and tea, enjoy them, have a chat.
Wk 3	• Selection of food. • Different brands (matching game, same products different brands). • Different prices—worksheet 'Tick the cheapest'. • Freshness—How to know when food is fresh—Fruit, veg, bread—discussion. • Sell-by date—explain this. Game—Find the sell-by date on a range of given products.	• Recap—Selection of food. • The layout of a shop, what departments are there? Fruit & Veg, Bread, Freezer, etc. • Make a shop poster, divide it into different sections, cut pictures out of magazines and stick in appropriate sections. • Procedure at checkout— Discuss the steps, role-play the situation.

	TIMETABLE continued SKILL—GOING TO THE LOCAL SHOP FOR GROCERIES	
	Wednesday 9 a.m.–1 p.m.	Friday 9 a.m.–1 p.m.
Wk 4	• Putting the skills into practice (with assistance). • Go shopping with Freda in her local shop. • Call at Freda's house, meet parents. • Freda was asked to make a list of 8 items required at home. • Find quickest route to the shops, identify landmarks, etc. • Introduce trainee to shop assistant. • Apply shopping procedure to this particular shop. • Assist Freda with her shopping.	• Putting the skills into practice (with assistance). • Go shopping with Jack in his local shop. • Call at Jack's house, meet his parents. • Jack was asked to make a shopping list in advance, 8 items required at home. • Find the quickest route to the shop, identify landmarks. • Introduce Jack to a shop assistant. • Apply shopping procedure to this particular shop. • Assist Jack with the shopping.
Wk 5	• Putting the skill into practice (with assistance). • Go shopping with Debbie and Paul (who live in the same street) in their local shop. • Call at each house, meet family. • Observe prepared shopping lists. • Find quickest way to the shop. • Introduce trainees to a shop assistant. • Apply shopping procedure to this shop (with assistance).	• Putting the skill into practice② (independently). • Go shopping with Freda. • Observe her as she shops for 10 listed items, assist only if necessary. • Take note of strengths and difficulties. • Go for a cup of coffee together, discuss the experience.
Wk 6	• Storage of food. • List the places where food is stored at home—cupboard, fridge, bread-bin, etc. • Discuss the difference between these. Worksheet—What product goes where? • Important points to remember when packing food in bags.	• Putting the skill into practice② (independently). • Go shopping with Jack. • Observe him as he shops for 10 listed items, assist only if necessary. • Take note of strengths and difficulties. • Go for a cup of coffee together, discuss the experience.

	Wednesday 9 a.m.–1 p.m.	Friday 9 a.m.–1 p.m.
	TIMETABLE continued SKILL—GOING TO THE LOCAL SHOP FOR GROCERIES	
Wk 7	• Putting the skill into practice② (independently). • Go shopping with Debbie and Paul. • Observe them as they shop for 10 listed items (assist only if necessary). • Take note of strengths and difficulties. • Go for a cup of coffee together, discuss the experience.	• Compare trainees' experiences of shopping independently. • Acknowledge trainees' achievements. • Revise any weak areas. • Ask trainees to demonstrate aspects of the skill that they were particularly good at. • Role-play—making an enquiry.
Wk 8	• Following contact with each home, set up individual shopping routines to be carried out on a weekly basis. • Plan a small party for the final session of the training programme. • Give each trainee a list of some items to buy in advance.	• Have a quiz based on all the information about shopping that was covered in the training programme. • Check if each trainee bought the items on their list. • Evaluate training programme with group. • Prepare and enjoy the party.

Step 7: Anticipate difficulties that may arise

In the course of a training programme it is quite likely that a range of difficulties, from minor annoyances to more serious disruption, will arise. If a little time is taken, when preparing the programme, to anticipate such difficulties and take steps to avoid them, a lot of time and upset can be saved in the long run. Even with the most careful preparations and anticipation some unexpected problems may arise. In Chapter 6 we shall examine ways of dealing with these.

When problems occur during a training programme, trainees often get labelled as being difficult, badly behaved, undependable and so on. In fact the source of the problem can often be traced back to poor preparation and lack of insight on the part of the instructor. There are measures she can take at the planning stage to avoid at least the more common or predictable types of problem. Unfortunately, it is not possible to give a list of 'problems to look out for', because they will always relate to the particular trainee(s) and the particular skill involved in a training programme. However, it may be helpful to use the following procedure for looking ahead, which suggests certain aspects of the training programme that the instructor should consider in advance. The process of anticipating and avoiding difficulties will be made easier if:

- The instructor knows the individual trainee(s) well.
- The instructor has examined the skill in detail.
- The instructor has some experience of training already.

The procedure

Now that the timetable has been drawn up, take a little time to reflect on each training session.

1 Anticipate trainee-related difficulties

Consider each trainee who is to be involved in the training programme. You should be familiar with their strengths and weaknesses and their individual personalities. With these in mind, ask yourself:

- Does the timetable really meet the trainees' needs?
- Are the demands that it makes on the trainees reasonable?
- Is it varied enough to hold the trainees' interest?
- Are you sure that each trainee genuinely wants to be involved?

If you cannot answer yes to each of these questions, there is a strong likelihood of problems arising during the training programme. There is still time to make changes to reduce future aggravation as far as possible. The following list of common problems may help you to identify any need for change.

DISRUPTIVE BEHAVIOUR

Disruptive behaviour sometimes occurs if the context of the training session does not adequately engage the trainee's interest. It may be too complex, passing over the trainee's head, or it may be below the trainee's ability level, causing his mind to be under-stimulated, resulting in boredom. Perhaps the session is monotonous, without enough variety or interest. In any of these cases, the trainee's concentration lapses and he may start to behave in an attention-seeking way or distract others while doing his own thing.

POOR ATTENDANCE AND TIME-KEEPING

This is more often the result of lack of motivation and effort on the part of the trainee than a practical obstacle. The key factor is the trainee's interest in the training programme and his understanding of what the programme could do for him. If the training programme is genuinely designed to meet the trainee's needs and wishes, it should be easy to motivate him to attend.

The point at which the instructor offers the trainee the opportunity to take part in the training programme is a very significant time. It is the best opportunity for the instructor to explain to the trainee how this training programme relates to his wishes and how it will help him to move closer to his goal or dream. Once the trainee understands this, he is much more likely to be prepared to make commitments when drawing up the contract (see page 121).

The time of drawing up the contract is the next key time in avoiding future difficulties. With the trainee well motivated, the instructor can outline the expected behaviour, time-keeping, attendance and other specific requirements of the programme. When agreement is reached, both parties can sign the contract.

At the first sign of the agreement being broken, the instructor can calmly refer to the contract. The trainee may, in the heat of the moment, claim not to care, but will usually step into line when reminded that to break the contract is to forfeit this training opportunity.

CHANGE OF MIND OR LOSS OF INTEREST

The same applies in this case. If the instructor carefully designs the training programme in relation to the trainee's hopes and dreams, she should make this clear to the trainee when offering him the opportunity to take part in the programme.

If this procedure is followed, there is less likelihood of the trainee changing his mind or losing interest. However, if this happens, the instructor must accept it and deal with it quickly so as not to spoil the atmosphere of the programme for the others. The clause that is included at the end of the contract is important and useful in dealing with loss of interest. This states that a trainee may leave the training programme at any time if he wishes, but that once he leaves he may not come back. If the instructor takes the trouble to explain this to the trainee in advance, there is likely to be less disruption caused by trainees walking out when the going gets tough or when they experience temporary frustrations.

LACK OF CO-OPERATION FROM HOME OR WORK

By looking over the timetable, the instructor will be able to anticipate any particular support or assistance that is required from the trainee's home or work. She will already have liaised with the family or supervisor regarding the training programme and have left the door open for further communication. If some new, unexpected, requirement becomes obvious, she should contact the appropriate person in advance of the training programme to seek their support. If the support is not available, the programme will have to be altered to allow for this.

Keeping in contact with the trainee's family where appropriate, and informing them of progress and developments, helps to promote support and co-operation.

TRAINEES PROGRESSING AT DIFFERENT RATES

This can affect group or individual training. Within a group, trainees may progress at different rates, inhibiting group instruction. In a one-to-one situation the trainee may progress at a different rate from that expected, requiring the session plan to be altered.

The instructor should be prepared for such eventualities so that she does not get flustered and time is not wasted. The easiest way to cater for this situation is to prepare some extra worksheets on the topic. These contain additional rather than essential information relating to the skill. They can be in the form of questions for the trainee to answer, puzzles to work out, tasks to be completed, and so on. If a trainee finishes the timetabled work ahead of the others or ahead of schedule, he can be given a worksheet that makes good use of his time. If progress is slower than anticipated, however, a small adjustment to future sessions in the timetable may suffice. In more extreme cases, a less ambitious version of the goal may have to be agreed.

2 Anticipate skill-related difficulties

Consider the skill that the training programme aims to teach and the aspect of that skill covered in each session. Having completed the task analysis, the instructor will be familiar with all elements of the skill. She should then be able to anticipate all the requirements of that skill, in order to avoid problems at a later stage. Reflect on each session of the timetable to check that all the requirements of the skill can be met. If not, the timetable should be changed now. The following list of common requirements and the difficulties that may arise in relation to them, may help you to identify any need for change or extra preparation.

WEATHER CONDITIONS

Where a particular training session requires certain weather conditions, it is difficult to make definite plans in advance. The best way to deal with this is to organise the training sessions with flexibility. Sessions that require certain weather should be alternated with those which do not. In that way, if the weather is unsuitable on a particular day, the instructor can introduce the session that was planned for the next day.

If the weather is a very significant factor for a particular training programme, then perhaps the time of year when the programme is organised should be a consideration.

There should always be a back-up plan for a training session that is weather-dependent. This should not be a last-minute time-filler, but another relevant activity from the timetable or one that has been designed for this purpose.

FINANCES

It should be easy to anticipate the financial requirements of a training programme by looking through each session on the timetable. It is important to clarify in advance exactly where the necessary money will come from. Some trainees may be able to contribute to the cost of a training session, others may not. This should be checked out in advance in order to avoid any embarrassment. For example, if, as part of a training programme in personal grooming, the members of the group are visiting the hairdresser, it should be decided in advance who will pay. If three or four trainees can pay for themselves and the fourth is being subsidised by the petty cash system at work, this will have to be handled delicately. The fourth trainee should be given the money discretely, in advance, so that he will be able to pay in the same way as the others.

The instructor should be quite clear in advance about the sources of finance available, in order to avoid disappointment or time-wasting in the course of the programme.

If, on reflection, the financial requirements exceed the amount that is available, changes may have to be made in the timetable. This can be done quite easily in advance of the training programme but can be very difficult once it has begun.

SAFETY

It is very important to consider the safety requirements of each session in the training programme. Accidents that occur during the programme can be detrimental and very upsetting for all involved. If the instructor does not have the resources to ensure the reasonable safety of trainees when carrying out a particular activity, then that activity should not be included in the time-table. No instructor can guarantee the safety of her trainees or give her word that there will not be an accident. Because of this, she should ensure that she has permission where necessary to carry out certain activities. If permission is required for a particular activity and cannot be obtained, the timetable should be altered accordingly.

Some simple safety precautions can be prepared in advance of the training programme to save time, such as a simple first aid kit for a home skills programme or identity cards for trainees embarking on a community skills programme.

EQUIPMENT

In drawing up the timetable the instructor will already have considered what equipment she requires and whether or not it is available. It is a good idea to make a list of what is needed for each training session and the dates on which the items will be required. This is particularly important in situations where equipment is shared. If two people plan to use a particular piece of equipment at the same time and neither knows of the other's plans, then one party is going to be disappointed. It is important, therefore, not just to know what you will need but to inform your colleagues and ensure availability.

Some provision should also be made within the timetable for unforeseen difficulties. Equipment has a habit of breaking down, getting lost or stolen or even being locked away and the key holder unavailable! To provide for such eventualities, it is a great help if the instructor has a back-up plan—for example, a 'floating' training session that is scheduled towards the end of the timetable but has few specific requirements and can be slotted in elsewhere if the need arises. In the case of short delays, extra worksheets can also be useful.

CO-OPERATION FROM PEOPLE IN THE COMMUNITY

Many training programmes benefit from the support of people in the trainee's community, but some really depend on this support. For example, if a trainee is learning to do his own shopping but has difficulty reading, he will need the help of a shop assistant. If a trainee needs specific help in order to be able to make use of his local library, assistance from the librarian will be desirable.

The instructor should identify in advance of the training programme exactly what support is needed and then check to see whether it will be available. If the community support is not available to the trainee when sought during the training programme, the trainee may be hurt or disappointed and unable to proceed. If, however, the instructor checks this out in advance, she may be able to find alternative sources.

It is hoped that, in outlining some of the common problems that arise during training programmes and suggesting ways in which they can be avoided, the instructor will understand the value of this process. With experience of running training programmes, instructors become more familiar with the trainee's strengths and weaknesses, personalities and the requirements of skills. Anticipating problems that might arise and finding ways to avoid them does get easier with practice.

Step 8: Draw up an agreement with the trainee

If the approach to training is organised and businesslike, the trainee senses that it is important and that he is being taken seriously. He is then more likely to respond accordingly, be better motivated and behave in an adult way. So far the instructor has:

- Set aside time to explain to the trainee(s) what the course is about and what it hopes to achieve.
- Detailed when, where and how it is due to take place.
- Given the trainee the opportunity to ask questions and give opinions, and incorporated these where possible.
- Allowed the trainee time to think about this offer and discuss it with others if he wishes.

Now it is time for the trainee to return with his decision made. If he wishes to take part in the training programme, then a contract or agreement should be drawn up between himself and the instructor. This may sound unnecessary or over-formal, but I have found that it works wonders!

The value of drawing up a contract is that both parties agree to do something and both parties are equally involved. Far too often adults with learning disabilities are in a position where things are done to them or for them. They are not called upon enough to contribute and give of themselves. There is great dignity in feeling that you have something to contribute, rather than simply being a passive recipient.

It should be made clear to the trainee that only with co-operation and the effort of both parties can the goal be reached. This is the essence of the contract. I am not suggesting that a complicated document with endless small print is required. In fact the simpler the agreement can be, the better. It can be called a contract, an agreement, or an application or enrolment form— the title is not important. The crucial thing is that it is a formal agreement between the two parties.

The contract should include:
- The title of the training programme.
- The objectives of the training programme.
- The dates and times of the training programme.
- A brief statement of what is required of instructor and trainee.
- Any rules which have been agreed.
- A clause to state that a trainee may leave the training programme at any time but that if he leaves, he cannot come back.

It should be signed and dated by both parties. A procedure

should then be agreed verbally, which comes into play if either party breaks the agreement. For example:

1 To discuss the problem.
2 To apologise if the contract has been broken and agree to go along with it in future.
3 To alter the agreement if necessary.
4 To leave or end the training programme if either party refuses to honour the contract.

This simple procedure empowers both parties to ensure that the quality of the training programme is maintained and that agreements are honoured.

The advantages of having a contract are:
● It gives the training programme a sense of importance.
● Both parties are equally involved.
● Both parties know what is required of them.
● By writing down details, confusion is avoided.
● It reduces the chances of rules being changed on a whim or in a particular situation.
● It helps to keep all parties in line.
● The training programme runs more efficiently.
● It gives each party the power to express dissatisfaction.
● It helps to avoid a reduction in commitment if the initial enthusiasm wears off.
● It helps to prevent people giving up when the going gets tough.

With the guidelines given above, a contract can be drawn up quickly and easily. The same agreed 'skeleton' form can be used for all training programmes with the specific details filled in for each individual case. See the sample form on page 124.

This type of form may be too formal for use in the home. However, I would strongly recommend that parents or family members draw up some simple agreement. It is even more likely in the less structured environment of the home that plans, made with enthusiasm, will lapse after a short time. A written agreement with a definite time schedule can help to avoid this loss of interest or motivation.

TRAINING PROGRAMME
CONTRACT

Title of Training Programme: _____

Dates: From:_____   To:_____

Times: From:_____   To:_____

Location: _____

Objectives:_____ 1. _____

                          2. _____

                          3. _____

                          4.

Specific Rules/Requirements:

On this Training Programme I will teach/learn to the best of my ability. I will stick to the rules that we have agreed. I will make every effort to reach the goal that we have set . I will attend regularly and on time and when this is not possible I will inform the other party in advance.

Signed

Date: **Trainee:**   **Instructor:**

I have completed or wish to leave this Training Programme and understand that if I leave I cannot re-join.

Date:_____   **Signed:**_____

Real Life Example

Tom was very eager to learn how to use and understand money. He was short-changed twice in quick succession and, as a result, his father put some time and effort into planning a training programme for him. The first aim was to know each of the coins and understand their value.

Tom's father set aside an hour two evenings a week, for one month, to work with Tom. They drew up a simple agreement stating what the aim was and the nights and times involved. The location of the training programme was at the kitchen table and other family members agreed to be out of the kitchen at these times. The agreement was signed by Tom and his father and stuck up on the wall.

All went well for the first two weeks and progress was noticeable. On the first night of week three, Tom was watching a football match and did not want to work with his father. When his father reminded him that he had made an agreement and that if he pulled out now the programme was over, Tom gave the situation more thought. He left the television and they worked together.

A week later, his father wanted to see a friend on one of the evenings that they were due to work together. 'But what about our agreement, Dad?' Tom asked, waving the signed piece of paper. They agreed to start a little earlier that night and then everyone was happy.

It is important to stress that a contract is only of value if the trainee really wants to learn. Furthermore, a contract that is signed reluctantly by a trainee will have no hold over him in the event of a dispute. When the trainee wants to learn, feels respected as an adult and understands what the opportunity offers him (and requires of him), then the atmosphere is conducive to progress and development.

So you have now completed the eight steps

This Lifeskills training is a complicated business, I hear you say! There is so much involved and so many important points to remember.

That is exactly how a trainee will feel when learning a new and

complicated skill. Similarly, this book is a task analysis of
Lifeskills training. It breaks the process down into all its elements, making it seem elaborate and quite complex. In fact, just
like any Lifeskill, once you learn how to do it step-by-step and in
the most logical sequence, you will master it. Practice of the
correct procedure will ensure that you become quick and efficient, whereas short cuts, which might be tempting, will almost
certainly reduce the quality of the outcome. Lifeskills training
should not be taken on lightly: it does involve time and effort. It
is better to achieve real positive change for one person than to
attempt a lot but achieve very little with several people.

6 Implementing The Training Programme

When all the planning has been completed, the relevant people consulted and the details agreed and confirmed, the instructor and trainee are ready to implement the training programme. This is the exciting stage when plans come into action, and the instructor and trainee work together within the framework of the carefully planned timetable, to bring about change.

It is at this point that all the benefits of the time and effort put into the planning of the programme can be clearly seen. The instructor can implement the programme with confidence and efficiency, sure that each trainee *will* make progress. The trainee who, at the outset, was assisted in deciding the direction in which he wanted his life to go, begins to see development in that direction. Genuine progress in a chosen direction is very satisfying and encouraging for both the instructor and the trainee and should be acknowledged to the full. Success, for which we all strive, is a powerful experience and perhaps the best motivator of all for future and increasing effort.

Over the years, I have implemented hundreds of training programmes. Some of these have been prepared hurriedly, without the necessary attention to detail or adequate knowledge of the trainees' real needs and goals. There is no comparison between the satisfaction of implementing a training programme that you *know* really hits the spot and one which was prepared in a rush, and can only hope to scratch the surface of the trainee's needs. Several times I have allowed myself to be affected by the pressure to start training and show results. This has caused me to cut down on the planning time, convincing myself that with plenty of experience I would be able to ad lib or fill in the gaps as I went along. I can state categorically that I never enjoyed or felt comfortable implementing a training programme that I knew in my heart was not well planned, and the desired results were rarely achieved. On the other hand, I have found tremendous satisfaction and assurance implementing a quality training programme and have shared a great sense of achievement when the task was mastered.

> **Key point**
> *The ease with which a training programme is implemented relates directly to how well that programme has been planned.*

IMPLEMENTING A TRAINING PROGRAMME

STEP 1: FOLLOW THE TIMETABLE CLOSELY

If a training programme has been carefully prepared, a comprehensive timetable will have been drawn up. This timetable provides the framework and all the necessary information for implementing the programme. The main task of the instructor is therefore to *follow the timetable closely*.

The instructor should follow the activities detailed on the timetable at the stated locations. She should keep to the agreed time plan where possible. This is the only way to ensure that all the necessary stages in the training process are completed. Some degree of flexibility can be built in to a timetable, so that if a little less than anticipated is covered one day, a little more might be covered the next. If, however, the time-scale proves to be unrealistic, it can be altered at an agreed stage (see 'mini-evaluation', page 157), to ensure that it is realistic and manageable.

When implementing the training programme by closely following the agreed timetable, there are some important points that the instructor should bear in mind:

1 Use an age-appropriate approach.
2 Make maximum use of allocated time.
3 Prepare sessions carefully.
4 Use appropriate language.
5 Be friendly, positive and provide enjoyment.
6 Deal effectively with unwanted behaviour.

Because of the importance of the above points in running a training programme that is respectful and successful, each will be discussed in detail.

1 Use an age-appropriate approach

From the moment the instructor walks into the room and meets the trainees, they are communicating. If the instructor is respectful and friendly she is likely to help the trainees to feel confident. If she is rushed and preoccupied this will also spread to the group. So, immediately, the instructor is creating or failing to create a learning climate. In *Lifeskills Teaching* Hobson and Scalley state, 'It is obvious, and research confirms that people learn and develop best in the environment in which:

1 They are respected, valued and regarded as important and significant.
2 They feel they are understood and accepted rather than judged.
3 The people they relate to are genuine, real people who are not playing a role or manipulating them.'

This is particularly important when working with adults who have learning disabilities. Because the ability of such adults may not reflect their age, they are vulnerable, often undermined or treated like children.

Respect for the trainee as an adult is conveyed by:

- Considering trainees' interests and preferences rather than imposing others' on them.
- Observing agreements or promises made.
- Listening actively and being open to trainees' ideas.
- Recognising and valuing trainees' efforts.
- Focusing on the positive rather than the negative aspects of a trainee.
- Sharing power—allowing trainees to make decisions and then act on them.
- Avoiding putting a trainee down or in any way devaluing him.
- Using people's names.
- Asking, not telling, a trainee to do something.
- Helping without taking over.

- Practising what you preach.
- Agreeing to disagree where necessary.
- The same rules and conditions should apply to both instructor and trainee.

We have already acknowledged many of these important points in planning the programme, but some apply more specifically in implementing it. The following are some practical guidelines to ensure an age-appropriate approach:

a   Do not make unnecessary rules
Enforcing rules will put the instructor into a position of authority. If the aim is to treat the trainees as adults, then all parties should be striving for an equal relationship. Some ground rules will be necessary, but if these are discussed and agreed at the outset, there should be little need to enforce them continually. Ask the trainees what rules they think should apply during the training session. Agree a few important rules and make it clear that they apply to the instructor as well.

Real Life Example

Fiona, a leisure club leader, set up a training course in self-advocacy, encouraging trainees to speak up for themselves and their rights. The trainees gathered at the agreed time and had to wait outside the club house, as Fiona had the keys. She arrived half-an-hour late and the trainees were freezing cold. One of the more outspoken among them said, 'Where were you? We're waiting over half an hour.' Fiona's response was abrupt and thoughtless: 'Look, I'm running this course in my own time, so don't tell me I'm late.' Fiona made a quick cup of coffee for herself and then decided on a topic for discussion. The trainees had to put up their hands if they wished to speak. She would not allow tea or coffee during the session. It was too awkward. Trainees had to ask permission to go to the lavatory, as Fiona did not want people running in and out. There was to be no whispering and no laughing, this was a serious session.

Having set the scene in this way, Fiona had already done more harm than good. Regardless of how excellent her course material may have been, she had already indicated that her level of respect for the trainees was very low. By introducing unnecessary rules, she was reducing the status of the trainees. By putting herself 'above' these rules, she was making it clear that she and the trainees were not equals. The aim of the course was that the trainees would feel confident and behave like adults, but her approach undermined their confidence and reduced them to the status of children.

b   Never talk about or reprimand a trainee in front of others
Always consider the trainee's feelings and respect him as an adult, even if at times he does not behave like one. Frequently, people who have learning disabilities are expected to behave like adults by the very people who continue to treat them as children. If a trainee is being disruptive, he should not be confronted about this in front of other members of the group or family. It is much more acceptable and age-appropriate to take him aside, ask what the problem is and see if it can be sorted out. Explain to the trainee how important it is to have his co-operation if he and the other trainees are to reach their goals. If the disruptive behaviour persists, calmly outline the action that you will have to take—that is, request that the trainee should leave the training programme.

As a simple self-checking exercise, it may be useful for an instructor to ask herself, 'Would I speak to a colleague in the same way as I spoke to that trainee?'

Always respect a trainee's privacy. Because of the nature of certain Lifeskills training programmes the instructor may come in contact with personal information. This information should only be used as an aid to understanding the trainee and his particular situation. It should never be abused to facilitate gossip or a laugh at the trainee's expense.

*c   No matter how simple the skill is, find an acceptably adult
       way to teach it*
Some adults who have learning disabilities have a lot of insight into their abilities and needs. They are often self-conscious when they have to learn skills which most people of their age know already. Teaching methods or materials which appear to the trainee as childish can emphasise the simplicity of the skill, insulting the trainee and making him feel more inadequate.

It may take a lot of courage for an adult to admit that he needs to learn a basic skill, and admitting this can be an important breakthrough. If the trainee is then made to feel small or childish he may be afraid ever to reveal his needs again.

Real Life Example

Hugh was 20. He had completed school but never achieved much. He now worked in a sheltered workshop and for the first time had a chance of a job in open employment. Because this was very important to him, Hugh admitted to his supervisor in private that he could not read at all. Up to now he had made out that he could do everything and rarely admitted to needing any help.

Hugh's supervisor wanted to help him and set aside time, two afternoons a week, to do a reading programme with him. The supervisor went to a book shop and the only book he could find at a simple enough level was a child's school reader. The instructor and Hugh began on the first page: 'Dick has a ball' and then 'Dora has a doll'. Hugh felt a bit silly reading this book, but when his five-year-old niece laughed at him at home, saying she knew that book already, he immediately pulled out of the programme saying, 'No one is going to laugh at me!'

If the instructor had anticipated what reading ability the new job would require, he could have begun with a range of 'social sight vocabulary'—words such as 'in', 'out', 'push', 'pull', 'canteen', 'private', 'danger', and so on. These would have been acceptable and useful to Hugh.

d Praise realistically

Praise and positive feedback are essential ingredients in the process of teaching Lifeskills. In order to be effective, praise must be realistic and in keeping with the achievement that the trainee has made. If praise is given too freely, its importance will diminish and it will cease to motivate the individual. On the other hand, if it is not given often enough, the trainee may lose heart and make no effort at all. It is important to find the right balance and the key to this is:

- Knowing the trainee well.
- Selecting goals carefully.

There is a difference between encouragement and praise. As the trainee is trying to complete a task and the effort is obvious, he should be encouraged with phrases such as 'you're making a great effort, keep it up, that is improving, you're nearly there,' and so on. Then, when a particular goal or sub-goal is reached, the achievement should be clearly acknowledged with praise: 'Well done, you've done it, all the effort was worth it, you're great.' Praise should not relate to the complexity of a task, but rather to the effort that an individual has made and the goals that are significant to him. For example, it may be a very significant step for one trainee to have learnt to write his own name. This might have taken a long time and a great effort, so it deserves enthusiastic and genuine praise. For another trainee, the same skill may only be a small step, requiring a little work, on the way to a more advanced goal. In this instance, the appropriate praise may be more low-key.

Do not patronise the trainee. This can be counter-productive, causing him to feel inadequate. Acknowledge everything that he knows. Often a trainee's knowledge or ability is inconsistent, but never presume that because he cannot complete one task he will therefore be unable to complete a range of similar ones. This may not be the case.

e   Acknowledge your own failings
It is important that the trainee feels on a par with the instructor if he is to feel free to make suggestions or give opinions. It is helpful if the instructor draws parallels between her own life and that of the trainee—for example, if a trainee is learning how to plan a weekend outing and feels childish having to tell his parents where he is going, the instructor can pick an example from her own life to make it more acceptable. 'It's the same for me or any adult. If I am going out at night, I always tell my husband where I am going and when I expect to be back, just so that he won't be worried.'

It is good to acknowledge your own failings, as trainees are inclined to think that other adults know everything. For example, if a trainee makes a lot of spelling mistakes the instructor can confide, 'I'm not a good speller either, but I found so-and-so very helpful'. If the trainee does something wrong and feels embarrassed, the instructor can defuse the situation by saying, 'I did something really silly the other day,' and relate a story that clearly demonstrates that none of us is perfect.

2   Make maximum use of allocated time

The instructor should ensure that whatever time she makes available for Lifeskills teaching is used directly for that purpose. The training programme that she is offering may be the only concrete learning opportunity the trainee has had that term or year. If the available time is eroded by bad planning, misunderstanding, interruptions, late starts and absences, the potential benefit may be considerably reduced. The following are some practical guidelines.

a   Be punctual and expect punctuality

The trainee will pick up very quickly whether or not the instructor is taking the training programme seriously. If it is run inefficiently, with the instructor arriving late and sometimes not at all, the whole sense of importance associated with the programme will diminish. Understandably the trainee's efforts to be punctual may then slacken and the training time in each session will be reduced, making it more difficult to reach the agreed target. More importantly, the trainee may feel that he is not being taken seriously and this could reduce his self-esteem and confidence.

> **Key point**
> *A Lifeskills training programme that causes a reduction*
> *in a trainee's sense of importance or self-esteem is doing*
> *more harm than good, no matter what skill it manages to*
> *teach.*

The instructor should agree the day and starting time with the trainee(s). She should require the trainees to arrive on time and ensure that she does so herself. In that way, mutual respect is demonstrated and none of the training time is wasted. This requirement will also help to foster an awareness of punctuality, important in many areas of life, but particularly if the trainee hopes to progress to open employment.

It is not uncommon for an instructor to insist on trainees attending a training session on time and then wander in ten or fifteen minutes late herself. This does a lot more damage than simply wasting some of the training time. It conveys to the trainee that the instructor is not his equal but his superior, and is not bound by the same rules.

b   Try to ensure as few interruptions as possible

When a training session is interrupted it takes the instructor and the trainees some time to get back to where they were. The flow of the session is disturbed and the train of thought can be lost.

Adults who have learning disabilities often have poor concentration. Because of this, every effort has to be made to hold the trainee's concentration for as long as possible and keep interruptions to a minimum.

Real Life Example

Carol, a woman in her late twenties, was doing an independent living programme with her mother. In the future Carol planned to move into a flat, and meanwhile she spent weekends in her sister's house, on her own whenever her sister was away.

One particular day, Carol's mother was devoting the training session to teaching Carol how to wire up a three-pin plug. Carol had a lot of electrical gadgets and did not know how to attach a plug.

They began. Carol's mother, Mrs Lynch, was demonstrating this skill using a hairdryer with no plug attached and a common three-pin plug. She explained:

Mrs Lynch: Carol, your hairdryer needs to be connected to the electricity supply to make it work. It has a flex (*holding it up*) but needs a plug to attach it in to the electric socket in the wall. Do you understand?

Carol: Yes, I know what you mean.

Mrs Lynch: This is a plug. Now I am going to open it with a screwdriver to show you what it is like inside.

(First interruption: door bell rings. Mrs Lynch answers the door and a neighbour wants to talk to her for a few minutes. Then she returns.)

Mrs Lynch: Now, where were we, Carol? Oh yes, I was opening the plug. There we are. Inside the plug there are three electrical connections, one of them is called live.

(Second interruption: a shout from upstairs. Carol's sister wants to know where her new blouse is. She's in a hurry to go out, so Mrs Lynch goes up to help her to find it. She returns five minutes later.)

Mrs Lynch: Sorry, Carol, I'll begin again. There are three electrical connections, one is called live, one is neutral and one is earth. They are always in the same positions. In the flex of your hair-dryer there are three wires.

(Third interruption: the telephone rings, it's a call for Mrs Lynch.)

Mrs Lynch: Oh dear, I'll be as quick as I can, Carol.

And so the training session continued. Carol had little hope of learning anything under those circumstances, and at the end of the training session both she and her mother were frustrated and confused.

When allocating time to the training session, consider the likely interruptions and the time at which fewest might occur. Steps can be taken to reduce interruptions by:

- Informing those in the house or workplace that a training session is taking place.
- Asking someone to answer the door or telephone and take a message.
- Putting a 'Do not disturb' sign on the door.
- Using the bathroom before the session if necessary, so that you will not have to excuse yourself during the session.

Even with the best planning, unforeseen circumstances can arise. Where there is considerable disruption it may be less stressful for all concerned if the training session is postponed and rescheduled for a mutually suitable time.

c   *Do not stray from the agreed path*
Once a timetable has been agreed and circulated the instructor should make every effort to follow it exactly. A review date will have been agreed to check progress and to make any necessary adjustments.

In the course of most training programmes, other needs will become evident, which also require attention. The instructor may feel inclined to address these, giving the trainee the instruction necessary to overcome the problem. However, if she departs from the agreed schedule the timing of the training programme will be altered, causing confusion. Trainee and instructor may lose their clear focus, get torn between different needs and fail to achieve anything definite. It is much more productive to follow the original schedule and take note of any glaring needs for future reference.

It is very tempting, particularly in the more relaxed atmosphere of the home, to agree to run the training session whenever there is time and for as long as time allows. However, unless there is a clear time schedule and a definite goal, training is likely to be haphazard and unproductive.

d   Always have an end in sight

Adults who have learning disabilities may have difficulty in relating the concentration and effort of the present to what seems like a distant goal. It may also be difficult for them to sustain an effort over a long period of time. The instructor should show the trainee that there is an end in sight, encouraging him to keep up the effort for an agreed length of time. Each training session should have its own small goal that the trainee can identify as one step closer to the main goal. The setting of small goals motivates the trainee, encouraging him to make the best use of time.

It is important to remind the trainee what stage of the programme he is at as he may have very little understanding of time. It may give him added incentive to know that he only has two weeks left to reach his goal.

Real Life Example

Gretta had undertaken a ten-week training programme to learn to write her name and address. The instructor knew that Gretta was inclined to give up easily, so she concentrated on making 'goals within goals'. The goal for the first session was for Gretta to write her first name on a line. Gretta had difficulty doing this and several times almost gave up. The instructor kept saying, 'Come on, Gretta, you can do it, keep trying, you only have twenty more minutes and then it is lunch-time. You'll be delighted with yourself if you do it. Keep all those letters on the line, you're nearly there.' When lunch-time came Gretta did have all the letters on the line. She had tried really hard because she could see that there was an end in sight and that she was not expected to keep the effort up indefinitely. The instructor was then able to acknowledge and praise her achievement and, although a lot of work still had to be done to achieve the main goal, both people went to lunch satisfied that they had reached their goal for that session.

3   Prepare sessions carefully

Most of the preparation work is done at the time of planning the programme and drawing up the timetable. However, there is some preparation that can only be done at the last minute.

In advance of the training session the instructor should look at the timetable and make a list of what is required for that particular session. She can then check the list to ensure that everything is at hand. Some training materials or equipment may have to be prepared in advance or brought to the room where the training session is located. The room may need to be checked if it has been used by others. Heating may need to be turned on or extra chairs brought in.

Certain people may need to be reminded of the session, particularly if the group is going out, to avoid any confusion as to the whereabouts of the instructor or trainees. The secretary in a work setting may need to be asked to take telephone messages to avoid any interruptions.

The preparation required before the training session depends entirely on the nature of the activity planned. In order to make maximum use of the allocated time, the instructor should refer to the timetable and ensure that everything is ready.

Real Life Example

The third session of a training programme on communications skills was due to start at 11 o'clock. So far the programme had been running extremely well, reflecting the time and effort that the instructor had put into its preparation.

At five to eleven the instructor finished her morning break and went to the allocated room. The particular session was on non-verbal communication—how to give and pick up non-verbal cues. The instructor had agreed with the trainees to use a video camera to enable each of them to see himself as others see him and to learn from that experience.

The video camera, video recorder and television had all been brought into the room in advance, but when the instructor went to play the tape she had filmed with the group, the machinery did not work. Half an hour of the session was wasted looking for someone who knew how to connect up the two machines. The trainees were disappointed that they did not get to see themselves on television and the instructor was annoyed that she had not checked out the equipment in advance.

There will always be the occasional difficulty that arises unexpectedly, regardless of how well the session has been prepared. In this situation the most important thing is to keep the trainees informed, explaining what has gone wrong. It is important that the trainees develop a level of acceptance and understanding, so that they can cope when things go wrong with their own plans.

4 Use appropriate language

Verbal instructions or general verbal communications feature very prominently in most Lifeskills training programmes. Even when using a good variety of teaching methods, verbal instruction remains very important as it is regularly used alongside other teaching methods (see Chapter 7). It is vital, therefore, that the instructor should put some thought into the language she uses, to ensure that it can be heard and understood. Careful use of language can favourably influence the speed and ease with which the skill will be learnt. The following are some important considerations regarding the instructor's use of language:

a Make sure that the words you use are understood
Consider the language used by the trainee. His use of language will be influenced by his personality, ability, background and the opportunities he has had to communicate with others. His ability to express himself does not necessarily reflect his ability to understand what is being said.

It is important to establish the trainee's ability to understand verbal instruction, otherwise you are in danger of pitching it at the wrong level. If the instructor's use of language is too complex and above the heads of the trainees, they will lose interest and find it very difficult to concentrate. It can also cause problems if the verbal instruction is pitched at too simple or childish a level; this can be under-stimulating and may come across as patronising.

Make sure that the trainee understands the words or terms you use. When learning a new skill he may require a range of new words, so the instructor should clarify what each word means, otherwise the trainee will not know what she is talking about. For example, some trainees were attending a class on making pastry. The instructor explained how to weigh the correct amount of flour, then said, 'When you have weighed the flour, sieve it into a bowl.' None of the trainees did what was requested. She raised her voice. 'Come on, girls, I said sieve the flour into a bowl.' It was not until one of the trainees said, 'What's "sieve"?' that the instructor realised they were not familiar with the word.

Key point
It is very important that instructors do not assume that a trainee is either not concentrating or not co-operating when he fails to carry out a given instruction. It can often be the fault of the instructor who has not checked that the instruction was understood.

At the beginning of a training session it is a good idea to introduce any new materials or utensils that will be used during that session, naming them clearly. When they are being used, check that everyone can remember the name. In the above example the instructor should have identified the weighing scales, sieve and other equipment at the start of the session and explained their function. When the time came to give the instruction 'sieve the flour into the bowl', she should have checked that the trainees remembered what a sieve was by saying, 'Has everyone got a sieve? Jane can you remind us what the sieve is used for?'

Where an object may have different names, always select one name and stick with it. In the selection of the name it is important to ask the trainees what *they* call the particular object and agree on one term. For example, an instructor picked up the item that she always called a potato or apple parer, and asked if any of the trainees knew what it was. Two of them said a potato peeler. They settled for that term and the instructor had to remember not to use the word parer, as this would only cause confusion.

There are several ways of checking the trainees' understanding of verbal instructions. It is not enough simply to say, 'Does everyone understand that?' The instructor may get a positive response but this does not guarantee that the instruction has been understood. She can check understanding by:

- Asking the trainee to repeat the instruction, expiaining any new or difficult words.
- Observing the trainee completing the task.
- Having a mini-quiz about the task that is to be completed.
- Asking one trainee to explain the task to another trainee or to the group.

It is important to build in a simple mechanism like this to check understanding, and to use it right through the training session. It is very frustrating for an instructor to realise at the end of a session that she has not been understood at all. Trainees may not have the confidence to interrupt to say that they do not understand, so they depend on the instructor picking this up.

b   Keep instruction short and simple

Many of us have a tendency to say much more than is actually necessary. When working with adults who have limited understanding and limited concentration, instructions need to be short and simple. Extra, unnecessary words only confuse the trainee more. It can take quite a bit of discipline on the part of the instructor to give just the essential information. Often, in an effort to be friendly and chatty, instructors warble on unnecessarily, leaving the trainee quite confused about what he is actually meant to do.

Real Life Example

An instructor was explaining how to iron a tea-cloth.

'First, take the tea-cloth from the ironing basket,' she said. 'It's a nice red and white one that matches the kitchen. This tea-cloth has already been washed and dried. I washed it yesterday in the machine when I was putting in some other things.

'Put the tea-cloth flat on the ironing-board. Oh, this ironing-board is a bit wobbly. I wonder why that is? Ah well, never mind, we'll manage with it.

'Make sure that the iron is set at number 3—that is the right heat for cotton. This tea-cloth is made from cotton. Does anyone know where cotton comes from? It actually comes from a plant. There you are, you learn something every day.'

I'm afraid that with instructions like those the trainees are unlikely to learn anything at all.

It creates a good atmosphere when the instructor is friendly and chatty, but when the time comes to give instructions for a task she must be careful to speak clearly and concisely. To return to the previous example:

1 Take the clean, dry tea-cloth from the ironing basket.
2 Put the tea-cloth flat on the ironing-board.
3 Set the iron at heat level 3 for cottons.

Speak slowly and clearly and ensure that you can be heard. Encourage trainees to stop you if they cannot hear or understand what you are saying, but do not depend on them doing so. From time to time do a spot check: 'What did I just say?'

Use as much variety and tone in your voice as possible, so as to hold the trainees' interest. Verbal instruction is liable to become monotonous and should only be used in short bursts unless accompanied by another teaching method.

c *Be consistent with the language you use*

The importance of agreeing on one name for an item and sticking with that name has already been mentioned. This point needs to be expanded. Lifeskills teaching, because of the instructor's familiarity with the skills, is often carried out in a very casual way. The instructor is explaining a task that she might perform every day and in which she has become quite automatic. Because she knows the task so well, she feels that there is no need to prepare clear instructions and so gives them off the top of her head. In the teaching of any task the instructions need to be repeated several times, and this is where difficulties can arise. The instructor may think that she is repeating the same instructions but often there is a slight difference and this can cause confusion.

Real Life Example

When teaching Valerie to make up a packet of soup her mother instructed her to:

1 Take out a saucepan and put it on the cooker.
2 Get a packet of soup out of the cupboard.

3 Open the packet and pour out the soup powder into the saucepan.
4 Fill the pint jug with cold water and pour this into the saucepan.
5 Mix the soup powder into the water, using a whisk.
6 Turn on the No 1 switch of the cooker up to 'max'.
7 Stir the soup all the time with the wooden spoon until it starts to bubble.
8 Turn the No 1 switch down to 'min' and stir the soup for five minutes.

The mother demonstrated this sequence step by step while Valerie looked on. She then asked Valerie to complete the task as she repeated the instructions. Valerie understood each step of the first demonstration and thought that she would be able to manage well. However, she got very confused when her mother gave the second set of instructions, because the instructions were not the same. Spot how many changes there are in what Valerie's mother thought were the *very same* instructions.

1 Take out a saucepan and put it on the cooker.
2 Get a packet of tomato soup out of the cupboard. *Which is tomato?*
3 Tear the packet and pour out the contents into the saucepan. *Tear it, why?*
4 Pour a pint of cold water into the saucepan. *How much is a pint?*
5 Mix the soup powder into the water. *Using what?*
6 Turn on the ring of the cooker to 'max'. *What does she mean, ring?*
7 Stir the soup with a wooden spoon until it boils. *How will I know when it boils?*
8 Turn the ring down to 'min' and stir the soup for a few minutes. *How long is that?*

This demonstrates how even slight changes can be confusing for the trainee. In my experience it is almost impossible to repeat a series of verbal instructions for a familiar task without making some changes. This is even more difficult if there has been a lapse of time in between. The easiest way round this is to decide on the simplest set of instructions and write them down. These instructions can then be repeated over and over again.

A set of written instructions is also useful if the trainee learns a skill at work and is going to carry it out at home. If the trainee has such instructions, those at home can see exactly how he was taught to do that task and can reinforce the same method, so as to avoid any confusion.

d   Facilitate the trainee in contributing to the sessions
It is important for trainees to feel some 'ownership' of a training session. If they are simply the passive receivers of information the atmosphere can become dull and lifeless. If a trainee feels free to contribute verbally to a training session, then he has some control of that session and is likely to have more interest in it. If the instructor wants the trainee to feel involved and free to make a contribution she should ensure that:

- Her own language is easily understood by the trainee.
- The trainee is listened to when he speaks.
- The trainee's suggestions and ideas are taken seriously and incorporated where possible.
- She pauses at regular intervals to allow or encourage trainees to speak.
- She gives positive feedback to trainees, thanking them for their contribution regardless of how valid it is.

Another way actively to involve the trainees' verbal skills in a training session is to put a trainee in the instructor's role where practical. If one trainee has acquired a particular skill, allow him to teach it to another.

Verbal skills, like all our skills, improve the more practice we have in using them. Too often, adults who have learning disabilities do not have enough opportunities to speak and be listened to, thereby developing the skill, and so a vicious circle develops.

5   Be friendly, positive and provide enjoyment

If the atmosphere of the training programme is happy and relaxed, the trainee will be more open to learning. Establishing a positive atmosphere, in which openness and confidence are the norms, should be one of the most important aims of the instructor. It is not a difficult task, and a small investment of time and effort can make a great difference. It is simply a case of concentrating on the positive, acknowledging the reality but looking on the bright side, being able to laugh at oneself and having something to give to others. The trainee should be asked if this is the sort of atmosphere in which he would like to learn. If he wants that sort of atmosphere he should be willing to contribute to making it like that. There are many ways in which this can be done:

a　*When implementing a group training programme, all the members should know each other's names and a little about each other*

The instructor should ensure at the outset that group members know each other's names. If necessary she could carry out some simple exercises in introducing oneself. Each member of the group should say who he is, where he is from and something positive about himself. Other group members should be encouraged to listen carefully and afterwards be able to identify the other trainees both by name and by the small piece of identifying information given.

Trainees should be encouraged to share information or materials and to help each other out where necessary. The act of helping another person can be beneficial to both the helper and the one who is being helped.

At the outset the instructor should explain about trust within the group and confidentiality, and how these must be upheld by all members. Trainees should be helped to see the needs of others and encouraged to compliment and praise each other where appropriate.

b　*Be positive*

Always focus on what a trainee has achieved rather than on what he still has to achieve. This is often just a matter of being aware of how a statement is phrased. For example, don't say to a trainee who is learning how to dress himself independently, 'So you are not able to manage to open and close buttons and zips and you cannot tie your shoelaces? Right, let's start with the buttons.' Instead, say, 'You are already able to put on a tracksuit by yourself. At the last training session you learned how to tell the backs of clothes from the fronts and today you've got that right. Well done, Paul. You will soon be able to dress completely on your own. Let's concentrate on opening and closing buttons today.'

Use as many of the trainee's existing skills as possible when working on developing a new one. If a trainee is learning how to use a public telephone, think of the skills he has and see how they can be incorporated into the training programme. For example:

- If he is a good writer, acknowledge this and ask him to write out the instructions for using a pay-phone.
- If he has good social skills, acknowledge this and give him the task of enquiring in a shop where the nearest pay-phone is.
- If he is dependable, acknowledge this, give him the price of a 'call card' and ask him to buy it in advance of the next session as it will be needed first thing.

c   Keep the focus clearly on the agreed goal

If the goal has been carefully chosen and a realistic amount of time has been allocated to a well-planned training programme, then that goal should be achieved. It is important that the instructor has confidence in herself and the trainee. The instructor should give a consistent message to the trainee, saying, 'You *can* do it'. If, for whatever reason, it seems as though the trainee will not reach the agreed goal, it is very important that the instructor takes action to prevent him from feeling that he has failed. This can be done by adjusting the goal to make it more realistic, but it must be done in good time and with the trainee's agreement.

Real Life Example

Sally was involved in a work skills training programme. Her goal was to be able to master the four separate operations of a new light-assembly job in the workshop, so that she could apply for work experience in a factory where that sort of work was done.

There were sixteen training sessions in the whole programme and it had taken longer than expected to master the first two operations of the job. The instructor knew that

Sally would only have time to learn one more. He discussed this with Sally, offering some alternative arrangements for learning the fourth operation in the future.

They agreed to re-define the goal for the training programme. The new goal would be: 'to master and build up speed, at three of the four operations of the light-assembly job.' By agreeing this change Sally and her instructor were no longer under pressure. At the end of the training programme they would focus on what had been achieved rather than feeling that they had failed.

d   Make the skill as attractive as possible to the trainee

Some aspects of the selected skill may be monotonous or of little interest to the trainee. If such aspects have to be learnt in order to reach the agreed goal, the instructor should try to make them as attractive as possible.

Real Life Example

Tom is training in the skill of attending a job interview. He will have to do some work on his personal hygiene, but is not interested in or motivated to work on this area.

The instructor takes time to explain the relevance of personal hygiene in relation to the agreed goal. She also incorporates a trip to the barber for a new hairstyle, followed by a quick pub lunch to make this section of the training programme more attractive.

e   Use every possible means to motivate the trainee

The most important ingredient in the entire learning process is the trainee's motivation. If he is not motivated to learn the skill, no amount of effort on the instructor's part will teach it to him.

The first step towards successfully motivating a trainee is to encourage and facilitate him in expressing his dreams and wishes for the future. Once these are identified and recorded, a long-term goal can be selected, and the more closely this goal relates to the trainee's expressed wishes, the greater his motivation will be. To make full use of this motivation throughout the long training process, the instructor should refer often to the long-term goal and how it will enhance the trainee's lifestyle.

However, the long-term goal can seem so far away that the student requires motivation from other sources in order to sustain his interest and effort. Here are some ideas:

1 List the trainee's achievements as he works towards his goal.
2 If he becomes down-hearted and claims, 'I can't do it', show him the list of his achievements.
3 Introduce rewards—'when you achieve X we will go on an outing/have lunch out/buy something new'. The reward should relate in some way to the skill and be of real interest to the trainee. If possible he should select it himself.
4 Give the trainee and his efforts your individual, positive attention.
5 Ensure that he understands the relevance and purpose of each task.
6 Break large tasks down into small, manageable tasks and acknowledge the achievement of each one.
7 Show appreciation of a trainee's efforts.
8 Seek his appreciation of your efforts. It is important for him to recognise the effort which the instructor is prepared to make on his behalf.
9 Remind the trainee of things he could not do before and now can.
10 Use any ideas and suggestions which he puts forward.
11 Introduce races or games of 'beat the clock' if speed is a difficulty with the skill.
12 Introduce an element of competition. This can sometimes be done successfully between trainees; otherwise a trainee can be encouraged to beat his own record.
13 Build up a very positive, though realistic, picture around the long- and short-term goals. Help the trainee to imagine the difference that the new skill will make in his life.
14 Set a good example by showing the trainee how hard *you* are prepared to work to achieve something.
15 Show excitement when something is achieved—it's catching!
16 Give plenty of praise, and make it specific rather than general. Instead of 'Well done', say, 'You were great to remember to . . .'

17   Inform other relevant people of the trainee's achievements.
18   Always keep an end in sight—'Keep up that good work until 11 o'clock, then we'll break for a cup of tea'.

f   Have fun during the training sessions. It is important and therapeutic to be able to laugh at life

A major factor in whether trainees enjoy a training programme or not can be the amount of humour during the programme. Trainees who enjoy the time and experiences which they share with the instructor are much more likely to want to make an effort and sustain it for the duration of the programme. Humour is a great ice-breaker; it can help trainees to relax and settle in to a group. If used appropriately, it can reduce tension and embarrassment and help to unite a group.

I often begin a training programme by telling a funny story about some mistake I made or some embarrassing experience which relates to the particular programme. Not only does this have the effect of warming up the atmosphere, but it demonstrates that we all make mistakes. Trainees should be encouraged to laugh at themselves and not to take life too seriously.

An element of caution should always accompany the use of humour. If used inappropriately it can be hurtful, offensive and derisive. Used effectively and for the general good, it should have the following qualities:

● It should be shared and enjoyed by all members of the group.
● It should not be at the expense or misfortune of others.
● It should not be based on subjects that offend the values of some.
● It should be well timed and not constant.
● It should not become hysterical or out of control.

6   Deal effectively with unwanted behaviours

It is important that the instructor should be able to keep control of the group so that all members feel safe and comfortable. Similarly, when working with an individual, she must be able to exercise control if the situation is getting out of hand. Throughout this book I have emphasised the importance of showing respect for the trainee as an adult. An instructor who draws parallels between her own life and that of the trainee, and acknowledges her own failures, will promote self-confidence in trainees and an air of equality and respect. However, if trouble arises with an individual, or a group loses its sense of direction or control, it is essential that the instructor should be able calmly and efficiently to take the reins and guide the situation back into line. Disruption should be identified and dealt with quickly, nipped in the bud, before it gets out of hand.

Although the primary objective of Lifeskills training is helping people to learn new skills or make better use of the skills they already have, sometimes there is a need to learn *not* to use certain behaviours. Behaviours which are dangerous to the trainees themselves or to others, which interfere with skill development or cause excessive annoyance or discomfort to other people, should where possible be eliminated.

These constraints on behaviour are not, of course, peculiar to people with learning disabilities: they apply to us all. People who want to live in a society have to take account of the needs and rights of others and conform to that society's rules or else face the consequences. With increasing and welcome recognition of the rights of people with learning disabilities, those working closely with them are often reluctant to do anything which might infringe these rights. Nevertheless, they need to help the trainee to control behaviours which are unacceptable.

The instructor should begin by exploring all positive methods of dealing with the disruptive behaviour. If none of these is successful, and only if the behaviour is sufficiently serious to warrant it, she should use aversive techniques. Aversive techniques are those in which some unpleasant consequence follows the behaviour, such as having to leave the programme or being denied some privilege.

a   Look closely at the unwanted behaviour

What is the problem? What actually happens? Can you describe the behaviour and the frequency with which it occurs? For example, does the trainee often behave like that or is it just on some occasions with certain people, in certain places, doing certain activities? Describe the effects of the unwanted behaviour on:

YOURSELF. How do you respond and behave? Would any change in your behaviour help at all?

OTHER GROUP MEMBERS. Does the unwanted behaviour affect them? How? Are they in any way provoking or contributing to this behaviour?

THE GROUP TASK. Does the unwanted behaviour prevent the group achieving its task? Is it more an irritation than a hindrance?

THE INDIVIDUAL HIMSELF. Is the trainee gaining or losing by the behaviour? There is usually a pay-off for all behaviour, although it may not be immediately obvious. Punishment, although negative, can reinforce attention-seeking behaviour by giving attention. If we can recognise the 'pay-offs' which motivate the unwanted behaviour, it may be possible to offer these for good behaviour instead.

Only by examining the unwanted behaviour and its effects can the instructor be clear about exactly what is required.

b   Speak privately to the individual trainee
- The instructor should be able to explain to the trainee exactly what he is required to change.
- The trainee should be offered an opportunity to comment, explain or discuss the situation.
- The instructor should offer help in changing that behaviour by making specific and helpful suggestions. She should be prepared to change her own behaviour towards the student if necessary.
- The instructor should encourage the rest of the group to be supportive.
- The instructor should identify what would motivate the trainee to make this change.

c   Draw up an agreement
It may clarify what change is required, and give added motivation to make that change, if instructor and trainee draw up a simple agreement. This should state who is required to do what, when and where. The objective of the exercise should be stated clearly, a date agreed to review progress and a method of reinforcing the desired behaviour decided.

Once the unwanted behaviour has been dealt with in this or

some similar way, the trainee should be better motivated to change. However, this is not always the case. If the disruptive behaviour continues, adversely affecting the welfare of the other trainees or the likelihood of reaching the agreed goal, it may be necessary to exclude that trainee. The instructor should then give the trainee specific information, identifying how and under what conditions he may rejoin the training programme.

The following is a range of typical unwanted behaviours, with suggestions as to how an instructor might deal with them:

A TRAINEE WHO IS EASILY DISTRACTED AND DISTRACTS OTHERS
- Remove potential sources of distraction—for example, seat the trainee with his back to the window.
- Keep the trainee as active as possible.
- Introduce as wide a variety of activities as possible.
- Place the trainee in a group which is unlikely to reinforce or welcome distraction.
- Confront the problem and permit other trainees to express their annoyance in a controlled way—appropriate peer pressure can be very effective.

A TRAINEE WHO IS VERY SHY AND WILL NOT JOIN IN
- Place him in a group with friends or other quiet trainees.
- Acknowledge tasks which the trainee can do.
- Seek the trainee's help and advice in areas in which he is skilled.
- Build his confidence by supporting and encouraging his efforts.

A TRAINEE WHOSE ATTENDANCE AND TIME-KEEPING ARE PERSISTENTLY BAD
- Remind the trainee what is required of him and refer back to the contract and to his goal.
- Give the trainee a special responsibility which makes him feel important and necessitates his being in on time.
- Point out some particularly enjoyable or rewarding activity which he missed by being late.
- Acknowledge verbally, or on some kind of chart, when attendance and time-keeping are good.

A TRAINEE WHO IS BORED OR HAS LOST INTEREST

- Remind the trainee that attendance is optional.
- Vary the activities.
- Identify teaching methods or materials which he particularly enjoys and introduce these.
- Give him a special responsibility.
- Acknowledge and respond to any signs of interest.
- Introduce new short-term goals.
- Talk to the trainee, ask him why he is bored and listen carefully to his response.
- Remind him of the agreed long-term goal and how it relates to his future.

A TRAINEE WHO IS TOO TALKATIVE AND INTERRUPTS A LOT

- Explain the effect of this behaviour on others.
- Put a time limit on trainees' contributions.
- Insist on others getting an uninterrupted opportunity to speak.
- Praise him at quiet times.
- Give him special listening tasks—'Listen carefully to what I have to say and then repeat it'.
- Give him the job of writing up notes or points on a flip chart.
- Avoid eye contact.

A TRAINEE WHO WILL NOT SIT DOWN OR STAY STILL

- Include as much activity as possible.
- Make reasonable demands of the trainee and praise all noticeable efforts.
- Send the trainee on errands.
- Introduce very short-term goals to increase motivation.
- Position the trainee close beside you so that you can reinforce good behaviour easily and regularly.
- Introduce attractive activities which require trainees to be seated.

A TRAINEE WHO IS AGGRESSIVE

- Identify what causes the aggression.
- Remove any cause of aggression where possible or reasonable.
- Refer to the contract which outlines acceptable behaviour.

- Give the trainee opportunities to speak and express his frustration appropriately.
- Forbid damage to other people or the surroundings and respond immediately if this occurs.
- Introduce relaxation techniques or activities which induce passivity.
- Give the trainee a responsibility which involves care or sensitivity, such as helping someone with a physical disability.
- Explain methods of self-control—for example, counting slowly to ten.
- Praise any evidence of control.

STEP 2: EVALUATE THE TRAINING PROGRAMME, GENERALISE THE SKILL AND MAKE RECOMMENDATIONS

Evaluation

Evaluation is an essential part of implementing a training programme, it assesses its value. There is a common misconception that evaluation only takes place at the end of the programme; in fact, it should be carried out informally all the way through. Honest evaluation is often resisted by the instructor, particularly if she is not confident of the quality of the training programme. The process can be threatening for both trainee and instructor as it may reveal that no progress is being made—none of us likes to discover this! However, the more carefully designed the training programme is, and the earlier the evaluation process begins, the more likely it is to reveal positive findings.

The learning process relies very much on the amount and quality of feedback the student receives. There are several different sources for this: the end-product, reaction from other group members or praise from outsiders. However, the main source is feedback from the instructor and specific feedback requires evaluation. It is essential, therefore, that evaluation should be seen as a thread running through the whole process. 'Mini-evaluations' should take place after each training session. Evaluation serves two main purposes:

1 It enables the trainee to check or be made aware of his own progress. He should always know where he stands in relation

to the short-, medium- and long-term goals which he agreed
with his instructor.

2   It provides feedback on the content and effectiveness of the
    programme so that the instructor can adjust it where neces-
    sary.

Evaluation is made easier and more meaningful if it relates to the
instructor's specific objectives in designing the training session
and, in turn, the whole programme. As stated in the section of
Chapter 5 on drawing up a timetable (see page 102), each
training session should be complete in itself and have clear
objectives.

When objectives are identified, criteria for success must also
be decided. Both the objectives and the criteria should be made
clear to the trainee and agreed by him. It is helpful to jot down
the objectives and criteria on the 'session plan' which already
contains notes regarding equipment required, breakdown of
time and so on. These facilities lead to an accurate evaluation at
the end of each session.

Ending a training session

When approaching the end of a training session the instructor
should wind the session gently to a close. Time should be
devoted to tying up loose ends so that the task, or a stage of it,
can be completed. It should not be a case of:

'All right, stop what you're doing now, it's time for lunch.'

'But I haven't fin . . .'

'It doesn't matter, it's time for lunch, you can finish it another
time.'

Instead, the trainees should be informed, when they still have
fifteen or twenty minutes left, that the training session is coming
to an end. Each of them should be helped to complete a
particular stage so that, even if the goal is not reached, they have
achieved something definite. The instructor might say something
like this:

'Now, it's twenty to one and we're due to finish at one o'clock.
You've all worked very hard today . . . Alex, you've almost
finished that worksheet, well done. Joe, if you finish the first
worksheet, I will explain how to do the second one and you
might do it at home tonight? Claire, you're especially quick

today, you've finished already. That's great. Could you help out by tidying up the equipment we were using and putting it away, then for the last ten minutes we'll have a look at how we got on today and what our plans are for the next day.'

Every session should finish on a positive note. Even if the instructor and trainees are disappointed with what has been achieved, the instructor should find some positive feature to identify. This will have an encouraging and reinforcing effect on the trainees: they will leave happy and be more inclined to return motivated to continue.

'Mini-evaluation'

Before the training session finishes, the instructor and trainee should set aside some time together to consider whether or not the objectives of that session have been met. This involves a quick check of the written objectives and criteria and some open, honest discussion. If the objectives have been met, this should be fully acknowledged and all efforts praised appropriately. If some have been met and others have not, concentrate on the positive, identifying what has been achieved. The instructor should then examine the objectives which were not met. She should try to work out why this was the case and incorporate the information into the next session or make necessary adjustments.

Because there is some flexibility in a timetable, small adjustments can be made and incorporated without changing the structure of the whole timetable. Sometimes it is not possible to fit in all that has been planned for a training session; at others the activities will finish ahead of time. A small amount of juggling of activities will balance this out. If, however, the training programme is really not running to schedule and the timetable can no longer be followed, the whole programme will have to be reviewed. A review can be carried out when necessary or at a set date, usually midway through the programme. A review of the timetable involves looking back over the programme with the trainee and:

- Identifying whether or not objectives have been met.
- If not, identifying the reasons.
- Taking note of any positive developments.
- Agreeing new and realistic objectives.

- Adjusting the timetable accordingly.

It is very common in programme planning to set unrealistic objectives or to include too much in a timetable, particularly for those without prior experience. If the instructor persists with an unsuitable timetable, both she and the trainee will end up dissatisfied. If, however, the objectives and the timetable are reviewed when necessary, or as a matter of course, the programme and the potential benefit can be saved. It is better, even reluctantly, to accept that a goal is unrealistic when this becomes obvious. A new, more limited goal should then be agreed and should become the new focus with no further reference to the original one. The new goal will be realistic and attainable, so facilitating the experience of success. If, on the other hand, the instructor and trainee plod on blindly towards a goal which will clearly not be reached, their efforts can only result in disappointment and feelings of inadequacy.

Real Life Example

Una was 28. She had a serious weight problem which, in her own words, 'was ruining her life'. She could hardly walk up stairs without having to sit down for a rest halfway up. Her choice of clothes was drastically reduced because of her size, she couldn't find anything fashionable to fit her. She felt so big and ugly! In fact Una was a very attractive woman with lovely hair and facial features, but she was greatly overweight. This was having a very negative effect on her confidence and self-image.

Una's mother agreed to set up a weight-losing programme with her, giving her every possible support and encouragement. Together they put a lot of work into drawing up a three-month programme for losing weight. This included a fat-reduced but healthy diet, a daily programme of exercise and a weekly weigh-in with weight recorded on a chart. Una's target was to lose three stone in weight and to achieve this she needed to lose three or four pounds every week—one stone per month.

For every stone that Una lost, her mother agreed to plan an outing for them to the cinema, one of Una's favourite activities. When the final target was reached, they would go to town where Una would buy an entire new fashionable outfit of her choice and have a trip to the hairdresser.

Objective: That Una would lose three stone in weight in three months.

Criteria: According to the bathroom scales her weight would reduce from 13 stone 7lbs to 10 stone 7lbs at the rate of 3–4 lbs each week, one stone per month.

Rewards: Weight loss praised and charted. For loss of each stone, a visit to the pictures. For loss of three stone, a visit to town for a new outfit.

Una was determined and the training programme got off to a great start, losing:

The first week—6 lbs
The second week—4 lbs
The third week—2 lbs
The fourth week—2 lbs

Evaluating the programme so far, they were still on target although the rate of weight loss was slowing down. She had lost one stone in the first month. They thoroughly enjoyed their outing to the pictures.

Una started the second month of the programme (if her mother had observed the pattern of weight loss and interpreted the signs she should have realised that the goal for the second month was unrealistic). She lost:

The first week—3 lbs
The second week—2 lbs
The third week—1 lb
The fourth week—2 lbs

Una was bitterly disappointed. The fact that she had lost a further half-stone was of little interest to her—she had not reached her goal. She felt so miserable that she went on an eating binge, eating a range of foods that were outlawed by her diet! She felt terrible after this. Una and her mother then had a good chat:

Mother: Una, I've been reading a diet book and in fact we made a very silly mistake. The book says that people on diets do not lose weight at the same

	rate all through the diet; the rate always slows down, with the most dramatic loss in the first few weeks.
Una:	So that happens to other people too?
Mother:	Yes, it says so in the book. In fact the rate at which you are losing is faster than average, so well done!
Una:	But I'll never make the three stone in three months.
Mother:	No, I think you're right. Let's make a more realistic goal, it will just mean you keeping up the effort for a bit longer. If you could aim to lose half a stone per month, that is approximately two pounds per week, and extend the programme for two more months.
Una:	Then what about the pictures?
Mother:	We will change that, too. We'll go to the pictures for every half-stone you lose.
Una:	Great, and the new outfit?
Mother:	Yes that is the final reward when your weight is down to 10½ stone.

The programme was adjusted with new, realistic goals. Una felt happy and was well motivated to reach her target.

Ending the training programme

Just as when ending a training session, the instructor should ensure that the training programme progresses smoothly to a positive end. She should ensure that:

- The trainee is always aware how many sessions are left and what has to be achieved within them.
- Goals have been adjusted where necessary to ensure a sense of achievement.
- Time is set aside for the trainee to ask questions or clarify anything about which he is unsure.
- The trainee should be clear exactly what has been achieved (see methods of evaluation, below).
- The trainee should know how and where to use the newly acquired skill and how it will enhance his life (see generalisation, page 165).

- The trainee should see how this skill relates to his long-term goal.
- The trainee should know what is the next logical step towards his long-term goal (see recommendations, page 168).

Methods of evaluation

The evaluation that is carried out at the end of a training programme should be more elaborate and specific than the 'mini-evaluations' completed during the training programme. It is the means by which the trainee and the instructor can determine the value of the training programme.

In carrying out a comprehensive evaluation, the instructor should:

- Decide what method of evaluation is most appropriate.
- Refer to the criteria for success which were detailed when setting objectives.
- Decide on her sources of feedback.
- Decide on a method of collecting information.
- Identify to whom, other than herself and the trainee, the findings would be of relevance and interest.
- Identify the implications of the evaluation for the trainee now and in the future.

There are several methods of evaluation. The four most commonly used are:

1 Observation.
2 Formal or informal feedback from trainees.
3 Testing and assessments.
4 Checklists.

1 Observation

Clearly, the most telling indication of a training programme's effectiveness is concrete achievement which can be observed in the real world. The sight of a trainee getting on the correct bus, behaving in the appropriate way and getting off at the stop closest to his work is clear evidence that the 'independent travel to work' programme has been a success.

Similarly, a trainee who consistently, over a period of six months, looks clean and tidy and smells fresh, provides observable evidence that the 'personal hygiene' programme achieved its objective.

Observation of skills should take place in the location where that skill naturally occurs. It is usually carried out by the instructor in the real or simulated situation. Where appropriate, a third party such as, a relative, friend, supervisor or co-worker can be asked to help with the evaluation procedure, to observe and then record on a simple record sheet specific aspects of the skill which the trainee is learning or has learnt. For example, Susan has learnt to set the table for dinner independently. How many times did she do it this week?

2   *Formal or informal feedback from trainees*

Casual comments by group members, other trainees, parents and staff can give a very good indication of the impression made by the training programme. This feedback, whether positive or negative, can be revealing. It may not be very dependable as it is often received from people who are not involved in the training programme and not clear about what it involves or hopes to achieve, but valuable information may be gleaned from casual comments. The more accurate the information outsiders have about the training programme and its aims, the more relevant the feedback from them is likely to be.

The most important test of any programme is its acceptability to its users. If it fails this test, there will be no need of any further evaluation. Voluntary attendance provides an unquestionable form of informal feedback, in which trainees vote with their feet. Other informal feedback from trainees, such as their behaviour during and after a session, indicates a great deal about how much they enjoyed the session and how valuable it was for them. Useful information can be picked up subtly by observing prompt arrival, keenness to get started, and a range of relevant questions or, in each case, the opposite.

Trainees can also be asked to complete a simple but formal evaluation form. If this method of seeking feedback is being used, it should be handled with care. Instructors must ensure that the trainee is capable of completing the given form or that assistance is available to him. He should understand what the form is for, why the information is being gathered and how it will be used, and if he is to give an honest opinion he should be able to remain anonymous. The trainee can be asked to rate the programme on a simple scale or he can be asked specific questions to which a yes or no answer is appropriate.

It is important that information is formally sought from the trainee and responded to appropriately. It acknowledges that his role is central in the training programme. It is another way of showing him that his observations are worthwhile and his opinions respected. The following is an example of the sort of basic evaluation form which can be used.

TRAINING PROGRAMME

Evaluation Form

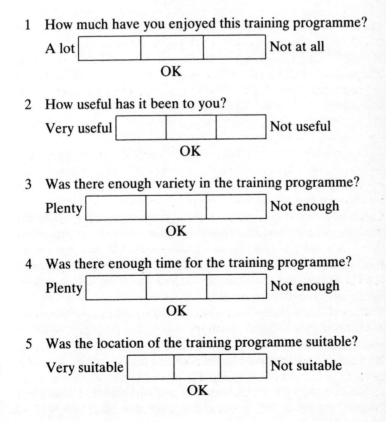

1 How much have you enjoyed this training programme?

A lot | | | | Not at all

OK

2 How useful has it been to you?

Very useful | | | | Not useful

OK

3 Was there enough variety in the training programme?

Plenty | | | | Not enough

OK

4 Was there enough time for the training programme?

Plenty | | | | Not enough

OK

5 Was the location of the training programme suitable?

Very suitable | | | | Not suitable

OK

6 Was the training programme well organised?

Very well organised ⬚⬚⬚ Not well organised

OK

7 Did the group get on well together?

Very well ⬚⬚⬚ Not well

OK

8 What did you like best about the training programme?

....
....
....

9 What did you not like about the training programme?

....
....
....

10 Have you any suggestions for improving future programmes?

....
....
....

3 Testing and assessment

Detailed assessments, which test very accurately whether or not each individual element of the skill has been learnt, are informative but can be very time-consuming. There is such a range of assessment material and pencil and paper methods of assessment available that they can take over the whole process of evaluation. Because they go into such detail and are so scientifically prepared, formal assessments can be threatening to instructors, making them feel that simpler, less formal methods of evaluation are inadequate. In fact, an instructor's own method of evaluation can often reveal more worthwhile and practical information.

Skills acquired may be tested in real or simulated situations. Video or closed circuit television may help the analysis and assessment of the skill performance and provide the trainee with valuable feedback.

A useful test of what has been learnt is to ask the trainee to teach the task to somebody else. This will give the instructor a very good indication of what has been understood.

4   A checklist

Drawing up a checklist as explained on page 75 and using it as a pre- and post-test (see Chapter 5, page 99) is a very effective method of checking the trainee's ability to perform each important element of the skill. It can be completed before the training programme, documenting the ability level carefully, and again after the end of the training programme. The sample checklist used as a pre-test on page 101 established what Ann knew before the training programme began. It then became obvious when the post-test was completed what she had learnt during the training programme and what she still had to learn.

The pre- and post-tests should preferably be carried out by the same person and, if possible, in exactly the same situation, in order that the assessment is as accurate and as objective as possible.

See sample post-test on page 166. This and all records of formal evaluation procedures should be carefully documented, dated and kept safely. The information should be available to the trainee and anyone who may assist him with Lifeskills development in the future.

Generalisation

Generalisation of a skill is the process of ensuring that a skill which is mastered in one situation can be transferred to, and used in, another.

The Lifeskills which we teach to adults who have learning disabilities are intended to be of real use to them. It follows, therefore, that they should not only learn the skills, but should be able to use them whenever and wherever necessary. For some people who have learning disabilities, the transfer of skills from one situation to another poses a problem.

CHECKLIST		
Skill: Going to the local shop to buy some groceries		
Name: Ann		

	Pre-Test	Post-Test
Can identify what goods are needed	√	√
Can write a list (or use symbols)	0	√
Can indicate the quantity of each item	0	√
Can work out the approximate overall cost	0	√
Can carry money safely	√	√
Can put on suitable coat	√	√
Can avoid rain or bring umbrella	√	√
Remembers to bring list	0	√
Can find the way to the shops	√	√
Can identify the required shop	√	√
Is familiar with someone helpful in the shop	√	√
Understands the layout of the shop—fresh/ frozen foods, bakery, etc	0	√
Can get a trolley/basket	√	√
Goes round the shop in a logical way	0	√
Can tell when food is fresh (bread, veg, etc.)	0	√
Understands the sell-by dates	0	0
Can compare prices where necessary	0	0
Can check list with items in basket	0	√
Can go to the check-out	√	√
Can behave appropriately with shop staff	√	√
Can ask for help if necessary	√	√
Can put items into bags carefully	0	√
Can keep cleaning products separate	0	√
Can pay the required money	√	√
Can take receipt and calculate change	0	0
Can put money away safely	√	√
Can bring shopping straight home	√	√
Can put items away in their proper places	0	√
Test(s) completed	15/1/94	18/3/94

Real Life Example

Peter took part in a cookery skills training programme in his training centre. He became very good at managing the gas cooker and by the end of the programme was able to prepare three hot meals. However, when he was asked to put these new skills into practice at home, he was quite helpless. The knobs on the cooker were different, there was not so much space around the cooker, his mother did not have oven gloves hanging beside the cooker as they were in the centre, and so on. Most people would adapt easily to these minor changes but for Peter the surroundings seemed to have altered the whole task and he could not cope. As a result, all the time and effort that went into the training programme had been wasted.

This kind of difficulty is common to greater or lesser degrees and should be kept in mind, as has been indicated in this book, right through the planning and implementing of the training programme. The instructor must always seek to ensure that the skill is learnt according to the method and circumstances in which it is going to be used. In relation to the above example, the instructor in the training centre should have made strong links with Peter's home to ensure that the cookery skills were generalised so as to be of use in his own kitchen. If it was not possible for the training programme to be carried out in his home, perhaps involvement of Peter's mother in reinforcing each skill at home as it was learnt would have helped.

However carefully we plan our training programmes, it is always possible that generalisation problems will arise because of a change in circumstances. A person may move from his house to a hostel, a new washing machine may be purchased which has different controls, and so on. If this results in the trainee not being able to complete the task as he had before, he should not see this as a failure or a backward step. The important thing is to identify the problem; then a small amount of extra instruction, which applies the original skill to the new situation, is all that is required. When a skill has to be re-taught in a new situation or adapted to suit that situation, the learning process is usually much quicker, as much of the original learning still applies.

Key point
When a skill has been mastered the instructor must ensure that it can be carried out in the situation in which the trainee will use it.

Maintenance of newly acquired skills

The beauty of preparing and implementing the programme in the way that has been outlined in this book is that maintenance of the new skill is almost guaranteed. The central requirement for maintenance of a new skill is that it was wanted and needed by the trainee and therefore will be put into use. A skill that is used will automatically be maintained.

Recommendations

It has been made clear right through the process of preparing and implementing the training programme that one skill should link with the next, in order to bring the trainee closer to his desired goal.

When a training programme is being identified the process is carried out with recognition of, and in relation to, the trainee's long-term goal. In the course of the programme, if motivation is flagging, the trainee is reminded of his long-term goal and how this skill will bring that goal closer.

When the training programme has been completed and evaluated, it will be clear to both instructor and trainee exactly what step has been taken, and what the trainee has achieved in relation to his long-term goal. It is important then that the instructor and trainee decide, *What next?* With the information fresh in her mind, the instructor should make recommendations in relation to future Lifeskills training. These might refer to the next logical step in the sequence, or the trainee may have other important needs which have come to the attention of the instructor in the course of the training programme, and which she recorded for later attention rather than diverting from the agreed path to deal with them at the time.

All recommendations should be listed, explained and filed or kept safely at some agreed location. This will facilitate future Lifeskills training and ensure good continuity.

7 Teaching Methods, Materials And Resources

If the trainee is to learn and make progress as a result of the training programme, then each training session must capture his interest and sustain his concentration. Every effort should be made by the instructor to ensure that the training sessions are of real interest to the trainee. Information should be channelled through as many senses as possible to heighten the trainee's awareness and increase the likelihood of retention.

TEACHING METHODS

The most effective way to ensure variety and interest is to include a range of different teaching methods when drawing up the timetable (see page 170). The teaching methods which I have found to be most useful and productive in Lifeskills training are:

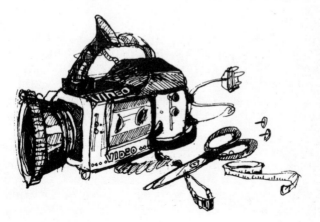

- Verbal instruction
- Discussion
- Brainstorming
- Written work
- Practical experience
- Video and slides

- Demonstration
- Role-play
- Prompting
- Games
- Quizzes
- Educational visits

The following pages will briefly describe each of these teaching methods. To make the descriptions more meaningful, I have selected one training programme and will give a practical example of how each method could be used in relation to the selected programme.

Training Programme—To develop safety skills which permit independent use of the kitchen

Background

This training programme is for a group of four adults. Each is able to prepare a cold snack for him- or herself and complete other basic kitchen activities. When questioned, none of the parents would allow their son or daughter to work alone in the kitchen because of accidents which had occurred in the past. These accidents were related to burns, gas, spills, cuts and fire.

1 Verbal instruction

Verbal instruction can be used effectively but only in five-to-ten-minute bursts. It is best and most commonly used as a means of introducing and explaining an activity or detailing what is required of the trainee. Verbal instruction without any visual or practical aid is demanding on a trainee's concentration and should be limited. To maximise its impact the instructor should speak clearly and concisely, with appropriate use of tone and emphasis.

Verbal instruction is most often used in conjunction with another teaching method, such as outlining the key points illustrated in a slide show, or explaining what is required of the trainees in completing a worksheet. Even in this context the instructor should speak slowly and clearly, checking to see that she can be heard and understood.

Example

The instructor used verbal instruction to outline the theme of a discussion she wished to have with the trainees. She explained that they were going to discuss accidents which could happen in the kitchen. She said that it would be very helpful if group members would share any bad experiences they could remember. She suggested some basic rules for successful group discussion.

2 Discussion

The aim of a discussion is to work together as a group on an agreed topic in order to reach a solution or a greater understanding. Within this group everybody's ideas and opinions must be valued and listened to.

Discussion is a teaching method which, in my experience, can be used very well or very badly. I have seen a discussion topic being imposed on a group just to fill time. On that occasion the organiser complained that 'they were a dull bunch with nothing to say for themselves'.

In order to be effective, a discussion must be structured with an agreed topic of mutual interest to group members and a clear objective. It may be beneficial for trainees to be aware of the topic in advance, so that they can gather their thoughts. Simple rules should be agreed in relation to discussion procedure—for example, only one voice at a time and keeping contributions brief. One member of the group should be appointed as a facilitator or chairperson to ensure that all group members get a fair chance to contribute. He should also make sure that the agreed rules are kept. Members of the discussion group should be present by choice and contribute voluntarily; there should be no pressure to speak.

Some people with learning disabilities can have specific communication problems which may inhibit their capacity to participate. A discussion involving such people has to be very carefully facilitated to ensure that each person gets the necessary time and help to give of his best.

A well-organised discussion, in which members are interested and feel comfortable, can be a great source of information. Members get an opportunity to share views and experiences and can learn a great deal from each other.

Example

The instructor facilitated a discussion on 'accidents in the kitchen'. The objective was to identify as many different types of kitchen accident as possible. She asked for a volunteer to list on a flip-chart the types of accident as they were discussed. The instructor explained that details of real experiences would add interest to the discussion and began by describing vividly a narrow escape she had had when a chip pan went on fire. A lively discussion developed and continued for half an hour. Out of this, twelve different kitchen accidents were described. This information would be used later in the training programme.

3 Brainstorming

Although this could be considered to be a type of discussion, it has a character and a function of its own. Brainstorming aims to extract a great many ideas from a group in a short time. Group members are encouraged to voice whatever thoughts or ideas come to mind on the given topic. The ideas are poured out in any order from any member and are not discussed. One member is appointed to write up on a blackboard or flip-chart anything that is said, no matter how silly or irrelevant it may seem. The brainstorm usually lasts between five and ten minutes, during which time nothing is censored or evaluated. At the end of the brainstorm the group can sift through all the ideas and put them in some kind of order. Then individual ideas can be challenged or discussed. Brainstorming is an effective way to get trainees thinking on a particular topic. It is also a good indicator of how much information they have on that topic. It covers a lot of ground in a short time, and as a result it provides a good base for further work.

Example

The instructor explained to the group what a brainstorm was and how it was conducted. Because of the speed with which ideas come forward she suggested that she should do the writing up. She then posed a question to the group:
'What would you do if you were lifting a saucepan off the cooker and your oven gloves caught fire?'
There was a great burst of response with more than

twenty suggestions, including 'call the fire brigade', 'throw the gloves out the window' and 'get a bucket of water'.

The exercise was very useful from the instructor's point of view. It indicated that the group members did not know how to react in the case of a fire, nor did they know that there were different types of fire. Group members enjoyed the session and benefited from pooling their information.

4 Written work

A worksheet is a page containing information relevant to a particular aspect of the training programme, which requires some input from the student. Worksheets can be developed in many different ways and can be enhanced by the creativity of the instructor. They do not necessarily require literacy skills and do not have to be very elaborate. They are useful for summarising a topic which has been covered, requiring the trainee to think back over what he did in order to complete the worksheet.

Worksheets are ideal for doing extra work outside the training sessions—for example, working at home in the evening to revise what was learnt during the day. They also provide a good link between home and work so that parents and supervisors can see what the trainee is learning elsewhere.

Worksheets can be made in many different formats. They can:
- ask questions;
- make true or false statements;
- summarise information given during the session;
- give information in pictures;
- outline a task for the student to complete;
- provide a relevant game or puzzle.

Worksheets can be used very effectively when working with a group. Each group member, while working on the same topic, can go at his own pace. With all group members busy the instructor is enabled to give special attention to individuals who require it. However, worksheets should not be used to substitute for trainee-instructor contact or be given out just to fill time. They should be drawn up carefully with a clear purpose in mind, and can be photocopied and used again. An instructor who takes time to make attractive and interesting worksheets can build up a very useful collection.

Example

Following a detailed training session on the different types of fire which can occur in the kitchen, the instructor gave each trainee a worksheet to complete before the next session.

The worksheet summarised the information that had been given in the session, using words and simple illustrations. It required the trainee to recall this information in order to answer the questions. It was a useful indication to the instructor of what the trainees had learnt.

Each trainee was given a file at the start of the training programme in which to collect all worksheets and relevant information. They were encouraged to complete the worksheets carefully, colouring in pictures and so on, as the files would be on display at the end of the programme.

5   Practical experience

As the name suggests, this method teaches through the experience of actually carrying out the skill or some element of it. Practical experience can be used right through the training programme but it is particularly useful towards the end. At that stage, all the elements which have been learnt come together, enabling the trainee to complete the whole skill. For example, if a trainee is learning how to cross the road safely, he may have spent time learning the colours, observation skills, the consequences of careless behaviour and various aspects of the pedestrian crossing routine; only then will he be ready to avail himself of the practical experience of using the crossing. The assistance which the instructor gives the trainee during the practical experience can be gradually reduced until the trainee is performing the skill independently. Where possible the practical experience should be carried out in the location in which the skill is most likely to be used.

In some cases the whole training programme is built around practical experience. The trainees are then put straight into the situation with total support and, in the course of the training programme, this support is gradually reduced.

Use of practical experience depends on the particular skill, the trainee and the resources available.

Example

Using the information which they had gathered during the previous sessions, the kitchen safety group had, with the help of an educational video tape, made a comprehensive guide of safety measures in the kitchen. The instructor set up the practical experience of a simple cookery session. During this session, group members would have to put into practice the safety measures—which were written clearly and illustrated on a large wall poster.

6 Video and slides

There are many educational video tapes and sets of slides available, which provide useful teaching aids. Showing a video or a set of slides which illustrate the elements of a particular skill can add variety to a teaching session. Information is being conveyed both verbally and visually. Trainees can often identify more with a situation presented visually than with one which they are trying to imagine.

With video tapes or slides the instructor can show just as much of the skill as she wishes and can replay it as often as necessary. Educational videos and slides on Lifeskills, which are commercially available, are usually thorough and well prepared, contributing valuable information as well as variety to a training programme (for details see Teaching Materials, page 193).

A video camera can also be used and provides an excellent source of feedback to a group. In using a video camera, the instructor should explain what she is doing and how the resulting video tape will be of use to the group. The opportunity to see oneself as others see us can be a very useful learning experience. Video recordings can be viewed and discussed at a later date with much more accuracy than memory alone could achieve. Video material taken at various stages throughout the training programme can also provide a useful measure of progress.

Example

The instructor borrowed a video entitled 'Fire Prevention in the Home', produced by her local Fire Prevention Council. She showed the portion of the video which dealt specifically with fire prevention in the kitchen. It illustrated very well the points she had made and gave very clear instructions on what action should be taken. The instructor replayed this section several times and then summarised it on a worksheet.

The instructor set up the video camera to record the 'practical experience' cookery session. The purpose of this was to put into practice as many safety measures as possible. It can be difficult to be involved in a practical session and evaluate it at the same time. Use of a video camera allows instructor and trainees to be fully involved in the session and evaluate it later. The trainees thoroughly enjoyed watching themselves and were very quick to observe each safety measure which was used and identify others which should have been used.

7 Demonstration

Many of our skills are learnt by watching other people and then copying what they do. Demonstration is therefore a practical and effective method of teaching. It involves a task being performed by a person who has already mastered it. When demonstrating, the instructor should be particularly careful about how she performs the skill. If others are to learn from it, it should be carried out slowly and in a logical sequence. The instructor should be aware of the key points of the task and emphasise these appropriately in the demonstration. Each movement the instructor makes should be clear and she should ensure that all who are watching have a good view of exactly what is happening.

People who have learning disabilities do not always know how to copy or may have difficulty in retaining the sequence of actions and then repeating them. There are two main ways in which this problem may be overcome:

1 By breaking the demonstration into small steps and allowing the trainee to practise after each step is demonstrated.
2 By prompting the trainee as he or she performs the task.

Demonstration is used to enhance verbal instruction. It adds interest and variety to the training session and illustrates clearly what the instructor is saying. In imitating, the trainee is physically as well as mentally involved in the process. The information is filtering through more than one of his senses and is therefore more likely to be retained.

When working with a group, it can be very beneficial to request a group member who has mastered a particular skill to demonstrate to the other members of the group. This gives due acknowledgement to the trainee who is demonstrating and provides interest, variety and added motivation to those watching.

Example

The instructor was explaining to the group what can happen if saucepan handles are left sticking out. She knew that this point would be made much more clearly and dramatically if she demonstrated it. She put some dried peas in a little cold water on top of the cooker, with the handle sticking out dangerously. She then walked by the front of the cooker, knocking against the handle and causing the saucepan to crash to the floor, spilling the contents. The trainees then knew exactly what she meant. She followed that with a second demonstration, showing how to clean the floor immediately and properly when a spill occurs.

8   Role-play

Role-play is a very active teaching method. It allows trainees to experience situations by acting them out and assuming roles within them. The situations may be based on actual or imagined experiences and can be used to reflect on or prepare for real situations which the trainees might encounter. In a role-play trainees can experience roles which are not usually available to them. Indeed, the same person can experience several roles in the one situation by repeating the role-play, rotating the characters. In this way a trainee gains a better understanding of the whole situation and its effect on others. Short role-plays lasting between one and five minutes are best, as the central theme and consequences can be easily remembered. Time is usually spent afterwards discussing the role-play and learning from it.

Many people feel inhibited and self-conscious if they are asked to stand up in front of a group. These issues should be dealt with sensitively, ensuring that no one is forced into a situation in which he is not comfortable. Time should be spent building up trainees' confidence and trust in each other through discussion, group activities and games before embarking on role-play.

Trainees who have learning disabilities may have particular difficulty in imagining themselves in another role or understanding the concept of 'pretend'. It is important to ensure that the trainee understands this concept before suggesting the use of role-play. He may be helped in the understanding of this concept if the instructor 1) chooses a situation with which the trainee is very familiar and 2) acts out the situation herself so that the trainee can see how it is done.

With a group whose members have a good understanding of the concept of role-play, the instructor can role-play a situation incorporating a range of intentional errors. The group can then identify and discuss the errors and repeat the role-play, demonstrating how the situation should be handled.

Role-play can provide great entertainment and this is a valuable addition to a training programme. However, it should be more than just fun: there should be a clear message to learn from the acting, the observation and the discussion.

Example

The instructor was anxious to impress on the minds of her trainees the action to be taken in the case of a fire breaking out in the home. She used several methods of teaching to reinforce this sequence of actions. She listed the four steps clearly to the trainees and wrote them in large print on a flip chart:

1 Alert anybody who is in the house.
2 Get everyone out as quickly as possible.
3 Dial 999 for help and give clear details of location.
4 Do not go back in for any reason.

The instructor then role-played the situation of waking up and realising the house was on fire. She acted out how she would respond, including an intentional error. The trainees had to identify the error, and this task made them watch very carefully. The instructor repeated this exercise several times, making a range of different mistakes. Each time a different trainee was asked to identify the mistake and then role-play the correct procedure.

The training session was thoroughly enjoyed by all and the instructor was satisfied that the message had really sunk in.

9 Prompting

Prompting means guiding a trainee through a task. There are three main types:

1 Physical prompting
This is when the instructor physically helps the trainee to perform the task, guiding his limbs through the action. It is particularly useful with trainees who have lower ability. If an instructor was teaching a trainee to butter bread she might put her left hand on top of his left hand to hold the bread in place. Then, with her right hand over his right hand to hold the knife correctly, they would complete the action of buttering the bread. Physical prompting accompanies verbal instruction and is gradually reduced so that the student can complete the task independently (see Fading the prompting, page 180).

2 Gestural prompting
Unlike physical prompting the instructor does not perform the task with the trainee. Gestural prompting indicates that the action should be performed and hints physically what that action is. Most gestural prompting is done with the hands pointing or miming what should be done next. Eye-pointing is a very subtle form of gestural prompting which may be enough to give the necessary hint for a trainee to complete the task. To return to the example of buttering bread: the trainee lifts the knife, the slice of bread is ready on the plate and he stops, not knowing what to do next. The instructor points at the butter and the trainee remembers the next step. He takes some butter on his knife and tries to butter the bread with stabbing movements but encounters difficulty. The instructor gives a further gestural prompt, miming a smooth spreading movement and saying, '*Spread* the butter on the bread'. The trainee imitates this movement and completes the task.

3   Verbal prompting

This is indicating in words what the trainee is required to do. It differs from verbal instruction in that it does not give a complete instruction, just a hint or a reminder. The instructor might give a demonstration accompanied by verbal instruction and then ask the trainee to complete the task. If he has some difficulty or cannot remember what to do next, a simple word or phrase from the instructor may be enough to enable the trainee to complete the task.

Fading the prompting

Prompting is used very commonly and it is likely that anyone who has experience of instructing or bringing up children is familiar with this practice. It is almost automatic and may not have been seen as a teaching method. In order to be most effective it is important that the instructor understands how to fade the prompting.

When we use prompts, our aim is to help the trainee complete the task so that he will learn how to do it independently. As he becomes more able the instructor should fade the prompts—the trainee does a little more and the instructor does a little less. Fading should be carried out carefully. If the instructor fades the prompts too quickly the trainee may fail and this can damage his confidence. If the instructor does not fade the prompting it may become a habit and continue long after it is necessary. The danger then is that the trainee may come to depend on it and this inhibits independence.

In my experience, verbal prompts tend to be greatly over-used. Instructors are inclined to talk on and on without pausing to check whether the trainee understands or needs this 'assistance'.

Example

The instructor had shown the group a section of the video on 'safety in the home', which referred to the safety procedure in the kitchen when going to bed at night. This detailed how one should ensure that everything except the refrigerator and freezer is turned off, remove all plugs, make sure that nothing is on top of or too close to a heater, check the smoke alarm and close the door. She then wanted each trainee to go through the procedure individually; she gave the others the job of giving verbal prompts if, and only if, the trainee got stuck. This kept the other students watching and interested. The instructor only intervened if the whole group got stuck or if incorrect information was given.

10   Games

There is an increasing number of educational games available, which can add interest to the teaching of Lifeskills. Games can be used to improve general skills such as observation and concentration. Card games and many traditional board games may be used for this purpose. Other games may aid the development of specific skills—for example, if an instructor is teaching numeracy, a game of bingo, either standard or suitably adapted, may provide enjoyment as well as helping in number recognition.

The instructor should not depend solely on games which are commercially available; with a little imagination games can be devised to enhance the teaching of almost any skill. Games can be simple and yet very effective, requiring the active involvement of the trainee and holding his interest. For example, three trainees were learning a new train route and needed to be familiar with all the stations in order to ensure that they got off at the right one. The instructor made a simple board game for the group. On a piece of card she drew out a track, numbering each square. At regular intervals she marked in the names of the stations in the order in which they occurred in the real journey. On the board game, in order to add interest, she also included some instructions like 'throw a six before you can move again', 'miss a turn', 'move on three places', and so on. The object of the game was to get from the start of the journey to the destination. Each trainee took it in turns to throw the dice and move his counter as indicated along the track.

Another example might be a homemade 'shop' assembled from a range of empty cartons, packets, jars and bottles, which can provide the necessary material for a range of games. If the trainee is learning how products are split up into different sections of the shop and where to find them, the instructor might ask, 'From all the items on the table, find me something from the freezer section of the shop.' In a group situation trainees can be asked in turn and an element of competition can be included to add even more interest.

Example

Having explained all the potential dangers in the kitchen the instructor introduced a game. She had drawn a large and simple picture of a kitchen and in the drawing she had included ten hazards, e.g. a spill on the floor, a sweeping brush lying across the floor, clothes drying on top of a heater, someone taking something out of the oven without oven gloves, etc. Each trainee had to take it in turns to spot a hazard. The group enjoyed the game and it provided another channel through which the information could be filtered.

11 Quizzes

Quizzes are particularly useful in motivating trainees to listen carefully and try to retain information. At the start of a training session the instructor might say, 'Today we are going to learn about . . . and I want you to listen very carefully because there will be a quiz at the end of the session.' The quiz is simply a range of questions relating to the information given in the training session. Questions can be made more simple or more difficult depending on the ability of the trainee. Trainees enjoy the 'drama' and the sense of importance of a quiz and the instructor should maximise this by arranging the seats suitably, selecting one trainee to write up the scores, operating rules for passing on questions and so on.

Quizzes also give very important feedback to the instructor as to what each trainee has understood.

Example

One of the first training sessions in the programme on 'safety in the kitchen' was naming and identifying all the basic items of kitchen equipment. The instructor knew that there was no point in referring to saucepan handles, sharp knives and so on, unless she was absolutely sure that the trainees knew what she was talking about. She selected the fifty most common items, many of which they already knew. She pointed to or held up each item, naming it clearly and then describing what it was used for. She then set up the quiz, the trainees sat in a row and one was assigned the duty of keeping the score. She asked each person in turn to name an item and explain what it was used for. The trainees' interest increased as the scores were being added up, one trainee was proclaimed the winner and the instructor awarded him a small prize.

12   Educational visits

An outing or tour which relates to the skill being taught can add interest and enjoyment to the training programme. While it may not always provide essential information, it can broaden the trainees' knowledge around the subject and increase their interest. Outings and visits are a particularly welcome break in a training programme which might otherwise be quite monotonous. A literacy programme might include a visit to the library or a newspaper office. A cookery programme might include a visit to a baker. Trainees who are learning their way around a particular town or city might visit and explore some of the important landmarks.

Going on outings also has the advantage of providing a change in surroundings and additional opportunities for the instructor to chat with trainees and get to know them better.

Example

The instructor was aware that the entire programme for 'safety in the kitchen' would take place in the training centre, so she wanted to include at least one outing when planning the timetable. She telephoned the National Safety Council to enquire whether they provided information to the general public. She discovered to her surprise that they had a permanent display of household safety measures in their showroom in the city centre, which was open to the public. They also provided a range of information leaflets and had a selection of video tapes which could be watched in their premises or borrowed. The instructor planned a visit to the city centre to see the display which was helpful and interesting. The group then had lunch out together.

TEACHING MATERIALS AND RESOURCES

Because of the nature of Lifeskills and the practical application of the skills, almost all important teaching materials and resources are made up of everyday things, people and places with which life brings us into contact. This book aims to help the reader to recognise resources and opportunities which exist in the trainee's home, work or community and to make maximum use of them. The location in which a skill will be used is the ideal location in which the skill should be learnt. This is not always possible and the instructor may have to create a learning environment which simulates, as closely as possible, the real environment where the skill will be used.

All Lifeskills are carried out in the home, work or community, some skills in more than one setting. Each of these locations is therefore a valuable 'Resource Centre'.

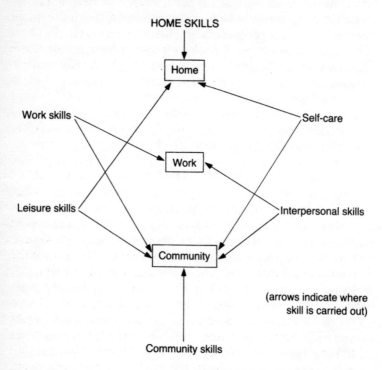

In addition to the 'natural resources' for Lifeskills training which surround us there is a great need for specialised teaching materials. Such materials will aid the training process by:

- simplifying the subject;
- adding variety;
- holding the trainee's attention;
- involving the trainee;
- providing relevant activities;
- stimulating the trainee's interest;
- excluding unnecessary information.

Most readily available teaching materials have been designed to cater for 'average learners'. As a result they are usually either too difficult or, when simple enough, too childish. There is a great need for specially designed, practical teaching materials for adults. Over the years I have been disappointed to find a very limited range of appropriate teaching materials for Lifeskills training.

Necessity being the mother of invention, instructors may have to develop their own teaching materials and should have faith in their ability to do so. Out of frustration at the lack of simple materials to aid my training programmes and to give them more variety, I began to develop materials for my own use. It started out as a series of worksheets which broke down various skills into logical steps. These provided the trainee with a range of interesting written and practical activities related to that skill. The trainees gave me valuable feedback on these worksheets which, with my own observations, helped me to identify those which were of most use. Gradually the range expanded. Colleagues and others involved in Lifeskills training expressed interest in these worksheets. They used them in their own work settings and the positive response encouraged me to look into the possibility of publication. After a long search—the field of learning disability being quite a specialised one—I found a publisher interested in my workbooks, 'The Lifeskills Series'. These workbooks are designed to assist in Lifeskills training with adults who have learning disabilities. To date three titles have been published: *Know Your Money* parts 1–4, *Improve Your Writing* and *The Time of Your Life* parts 1 and 2. Others are being prepared on Home Skills, Self-Care and Communication Skills.

I tell this story not only to inform you of the availability of these materials, but because I firmly believe that there is a lot of talent out there and many untapped resources. If you have prepared any teaching materials or drawn up useful training programmes, they may be of great value to others working in this field. If you have never developed any of your own teaching materials, perhaps you should give it a try! It may be simpler and more beneficial than you think.

The rest of this chapter will give details of materials and resources which may be useful in enhancing Lifeskills training. It will include:

- Specific teaching materials which I have found useful.
- The sources of a range of other materials which may be of use.
- A list of relevant Irish organisations.
- A list of relevant English organisations.

These materials will be listed under the six Lifeskills areas for easy reference.

1   Self-care

Unit 1—Heredity and Environment, M. Mulrenna. Social and Health Education Series. CDVEC, Curriculum Development Unit, Sundrive Road, Crumlin, Dublin 12, 1986.
This workbook contains practical information for discussion on topics such as 'myself', 'who am I?', 'my family and community'. There is a range of interesting worksheets for the trainee to complete.

Unit 3—Growth and Development, F. Ruane. Social and Health Education Series. CDVEC, Curriculum Development Unit, Sundrive Road, Road, Crumlin, Dublin 12, 1986.
This workbook contains practical information on physical, emotional and social development. It identifies changing relationships and adult responsibility. There is a range of interesting worksheets for the trainee to complete.

EASE—Essential Adult Sex Education. Concord Film Council, 201 Felixstowe Road, Ipswich IP3 1BJ.
Multi-media—teaching pictures, written material and films.

Teaching materials and programmes designed to teach basic information, responsible behaviour and self protection.

Having a Period, A. Craft. Camera Talks—Oxford Educational Resources, 197 Botley Road, Oxford OX2 OHE.
Tape/slides/booklet. The set introduces the subject of menstruation and deals with its management in a clear and sensitive way.

The Picture of Health A. Craft. Camera Talks—Oxford Educational Resources, 197 Botley Road, Oxford OX2 OHE.
Tape/slides/booklet. The set of slides deals with self-care subjects such as personal hygiene, diet and weight, sleep and exercise. It provides practical instruction and is very useful in stimulating discussion.

Sexuality and Mental Handicap—An Educator's Resource Book, H. Dixon. Learning Development Aids, Duke Street, Wisbech, Cambridgeshire, 1988.
A handbook which includes exercises on body awareness, self-esteem, looking after oneself, relationships, being sexual and pregnancy. It includes a section on useful resources and addresses.

2   Home skills

My Cook Book, R. Marshall. BILD Publications, 1983.
Book and teacher's notes. Contains clear and simple information with helpful graphics on diet, general hygiene, meal planning and preparation and food storage, also 100 recipes.

The Lunch Game, P. Noonan Walsh and A. Kelly. St Michael's House Research, Upper Kilmacud Road, Stillorgan, Co. Dublin, Ireland, 1989.
Game which identifies the four main food groups, simply and clearly divided. Gives background to healthy meal planning by means of a colourful and enjoyable game.

Unit 2—Healthy and Safe Living, M. O'Donoghue. Social and Health Education Series. CDVEC, Curriculum Development Unit, Sundrive Road, Crumlin, Dublin 12, 1986.
Book containing worksheets which provides information and facilitates discussion on topics such as personal care, hygiene, food selection, exercise, alcohol and drug abuse.

Watch out in the Kitchen, A. Craft. Camera Talks—Oxford Educational Resources, 197 Botley Road, Oxford OX2 OHE. Tape/set of slides/booklet. The 44 slides look at safety in the home, how accidents occur and how they can be prevented. Clear and easy to follow. Helpful for stimulating discussions.

Personal Safety—Lifeskills Manual, J. Robertson. Winslow Press, Telford Road, Bicester OX6 0TS, 1987.
Book/worksheets. A training resource including clear information and worksheets. It focuses on safety in the home and the community.

Sunderland Sequential Skills Programme, Sunderland Social Services. Nottingham Rehab, 17 Ludlow Road, West Bridgeford, Nottingham NG2 6HD, 1986.
Introductory booklet plus worksheets presented in an A4 ring binder, covering such skills as housework, laundry, shopping, cookery and sewing.

3   Community skills

Basic Skills You Need, H. M. Dobinson. Nelson & Son Ltd., Lincoln Way, Windmill Road, Sunbury-on-Thames, Middlesex TW16 7HP, 1976.
Workbook covering basic skills like form-filling, making decisions, finding information, following directions.

Focus on the Community: 1) Family and Housing; 2) Work and Leisure, B. Nixon. University Tutorial Press Ltd., Great Sutton Street, London EC1, 1977.
Book providing information, problems and skills relevant to living in the community.

Consumer Education. Consumer's Association, 1978.
A resources handbook for teachers. It includes a file of 64 subjects from advertising, weights and measures to making a complaint. It contains student activities and teaching materials.

Know Your Money, Parts 1–4, M. Macnamara. Wordwell Ltd, 1990.
A training package, each part containing 60–80 worksheets. Designed to teach adults the basic concepts of money.

Part 1: Number and counting. This part introduces numbers and counting and includes 50 worksheets.
Part 2: Addition and subtraction made simple. This part introduces addition and subtraction in just enough detail to manage money (50 worksheets).
Part 3: A close-up of coins. This part introduces each coin and note and explains their value (50 worksheets).
Part 4: Practical use of money. This relates all the above skills to the practical and safe use of money (50 worksheets).

Look Out, A. Craft. Camera Talks—Oxford Educational Resources, 197 Botley Road, Oxford OX2 OHE.
Tape/set of slides/booklet. The 49 slides deal with the subject of road safety, outlining things to look out for. It details the correct procedure for crossing the road. Provides good material for discussion.

Friends and Neighbours. Gloucester Health Authority, Torbay Hospital, Video Library, Medical Centre, Torquay TQ2 7AA, 1985.
Video cassette (32 minutes) concerned with the rights of people with learning disabilities, the process of normalisation and community integration.

A Part of the Community—Social integration and neighbourhood networks, D. Atkinson and L. Ward. CMH Publications, 5 Kentings, Comberton, Cambs. CB3 7DT, 1986.
This booklet looks at difficulties involved in social integration and practical strategies to help people to achieve that goal. Useful in promoting discussion.

Socialising—A discussion pack to build social skills and confidence. Learning Development Aids, Duke Street, Wisbech, Cambs. PE13 2AE, 1987.
Student worksheets and teacher's notes. This pack is designed to help adults make the transition to living in the community, through four real-life situations.

Behave Yourself, A. Craft. Camera Talks—Oxford Educational Resources, 197 Botley Road, Oxford OX2 OHE.
Tape/set of slides/booklet. The 42 slides present acceptable conduct in a range of everyday settings. These give clear instructions and provide useful discussion material.

Lifeskills Teaching Programmes, B. Hopson and M. Scully. Lifeskills Associates, Ashling, Back Church Lane, Leeds LS16 8DN.
Set of teaching programmes. This set includes eight teaching programmes, which include information, ideas and tips on each Lifeskill area. They list a range of teaching materials which have been tested by over 100 teachers.

4 Interpersonal skills

The Gamesters' Handbook, D. Brandes and H. Philips. Hutchinson, 1978.
Book including 140 games and ideas to assist the development of social and interpersonal skills.

Games and Simulations in Action, A. Davidson and P. Gordon. Woburn Press Ltd., 11 Gainsborough Road, London E11 1RS, 1978.
Book describing how to use games, role-playing to assist the developing of values and making relationships.

The LASA Pack (Learning About Self-Advocacy). CMH Publications, 5 Kentings, Comberton, Cambs. CB3 7DT, 1988.
This pack contains five well illustrated booklets each covering, in a clear and practical way, one aspect of setting up a self-advocacy group.

We Can Speak for Ourselves, P. Williams and B. Shoultz. Human Horizon Series. Souvenir Press, London, 1982.
Book that includes teaching materials, discussion and suggestions around the topics of rights and responsibilities. It describes successful self-advocacy projects and provides practical advice and support for their development.

Teaching Social and Lifeskills, National Extension College/ Association for Liberal Education. LDA, Duke Street, Wisbech, Cambs, PE13 2AE.
This guidebook offers a variety of practical teaching strategies plus a detailed guide to sources of ideas, help and advice.

Feeling Good About Yourself, G. Blum. Concord Film Council, 201 Felixstowe Road, Ipswich IP3 9BJ.
Video cassette/manual. Demonstration of interactive methods

of socialisation and learning. Gives ideas on how to improve self-image and promote confidence.

Role Play and Language Development, P. Herbert. CDVEC, Curriculum Development Unit, Sundrive Road, Crumlin, Dublin 12, 1986.
This booklet explains ways in which simple role-play can be used in the development of language. It gives a range of life situations and ideas for role-play with adult students.

5 Leisure skills

Give Us the Chance, Disabled Living Foundation. Town and Country Productions, 21 Cheyne Row, London SW3 5HP, 1983.
Video cassette (36 minutes) promoting positive ideas and approaches to recreation and physical activities and guidelines as to how to set them up.

Leisure, A. Wertheimer. Campaign for people with Mental Handicaps. CMH Publications, 5 Kentings, Comberton, Cambs, PE13 2AE, 1982.
Discussion document that challenges segregated leisure services and looks at the need and way to re-think future services.

Unit 4—Work and Leisure, N. Mernagh. Social and Health Education Series. CDVEC, Curriculum Development Unit, Sundrive Road, Crumlin, Dublin 12, 1986.
This workbook contains information for discussion and trainee worksheets on the importance of work relaxation and leisure. It gives ideas on how to make the best of leisure time.

You and Your Leisure, C. Adams. Viewfinder.
This book recognises the importance of good use of leisure time. It gives ideas for activities and methods of planning time.

6 Workskills (including functional literacy and numeracy)

Careers Guidance, J. Hayes and B. Hopson. Heinemann Educational Books, London, 1972.
Book. A selection of self-assessment techniques, aids to job choice and questionnaires.

PIG—Pictorial Interests Guide, T. Crowley. CRAC/Hobsons Press, Bateman Street, Cambridge CB2 1LZ, 1974.

Teaching package containing 54 cards designed to help discover interests and job preferences. Accompanying filmstrip and teacher's manual.

Setting Up Workplace Basic Skills Training, ALBSU special development project. ALBSU (Adult Literary and Basic Skills Unit), Kingsbourne House, High Holborn, London WC1V 7DA, 1990.
Book that identifies basic skills, justifies the benefits of training, suggests how needs can be met.

Creating Work Opportunities: For Europeans with a Mental Handicap, edited by P. Noonan Walsh. Lisieux Hall, Whittle-le-Woods, Chorley, Lancashire PR6 7DX, 1990.
A resource book which details rights, routes, realities, resources and resolutions in relation to work opportunities.

Getting Employed, Staying Employed, C. S. McLoughlin, J. B. Garner and M. Callahan. Paul H. Brookes, Quest Meridian Ltd., 145A Croydon Road, Kent BR3 3RB, 1987.
A practical 'how to' book filled with specific strategies for securing employment. Describes strategies for job development and critical employment training.

Supported Employment—A community implementation guide, T. Bellamy, L. E. Rhodes, D. M. Mark and J. M. Albin. Paul H. Brookes, Quest Meridian Ltd., 145A Croydon Road, Kent BR3 3RB, 1988.
Book which includes practical advice on implementing supported work programmes, describing the needs and perspectives of each party.

Functional Literacy and Numeracy: Improve Your Writing, M. Macnamara. Due for publication in 1995.
A training package containing 60 worksheets for the trainee. These worksheets aim to help the trainee make maximum practical use of limited writing ability. They cover the writing of name, address, simple greeting and post cards, letters and forms.

The Sum Life Series, P. McCarthy. CDVEC, Curriculum Development Unit, Sundrive Road, Crumlin, Dublin 12, 1989.
A series of work booklets, each dealing with some aspect of a situation involving specific skills. There are ideas for discussion

and worksheets for the trainee. The subjects covered are: Eating out, measurement, saving, value-for-money, time, using a calculator and discounts.

Literacy Workbook Series, P. Duffy and P. McCarthy. 1 Everyday English. 2 Reading and Understanding. 3 Working with Words. 4 Writing Skills. CDVEC, Curriculum Development Unit, Sundrive Road, Crumlin, Dublin 12, 1990.
A workbook series, each giving instructions and practical exercises on aspects of literacy such as punctuation, forming a sentence, building vocabulary, answering questions, writing a story, applying for a job.

The Time of Your Life—Parts 1 and 2, M. Macnamara. Due for publication in 1995.
Training packages each containing 60–80 worksheets in photocopying masters.
Part 1: Breaks down the understanding of telling the time into simple stages, giving instructions and providing interesting worksheets to practise each stage.
Part 2: Explains more complicated aspects of telling the time, such as the digital 24-hour clock. Measuring and gauging time, following travel and other timetables by means of instruction and worksheets.

There is a very comprehensive range of literacy and to a lesser extent numeracy materials available. The two main sources are:
NALA (National Adult Literacy Agency), 76 Lower Gardiner Street, Dublin 1, Ireland. (Send for catalogue and prices.)
ALBSU (Adult Literacy and Basic Skills Unit), Kingsbourne House, 229/231 High Holborn, London WC1 7DA.
ALBSU have produced an elaborate guide to material and resources in adult literacy and basic skills. It is very useful and comprehensive.

OTHER SOURCES OF TEACHING MATERIALS

Audio-visual materials

Camera Talks Ltd., 31 North Row, London W1R 2EN.
Send away for audio-visual aids catalogue which lists numerous

titles under such headings as Health and Hygiene, House Safety and Health and Safety at Work.

'Mediawise' is the Mental Health Media Council quarterly video directory (free), 380/384 Harrow Road, London W9 2HU.
Along with a wide range of topics it includes videos under the headings 'Children with Learning Disabilities' and 'Adults with Learning Disabilities'.

'Watchword' video specialises in training and promotional videos: 45 Hazel Road, London NW10.

Concord Video, 201 Felixstowe Road, Ipswich IP3 9BJ.
Free list—Mental Health.
Free list—Videos and films for the caring professions.

The Irish Film Institute, 31 North Frederick Street, Dublin 1, Ireland.
Catalogue of films and videos in different categories, e.g. Health and Safety. Videos/films may be bought or rented, many can be borrowed free of charge.

Suppliers of teaching packs, handbooks, readers, worksheets and other teaching materials

Further Education Unit (FEU) Citadel Place, Tinworth St., London SE11 5EH (Tel. 0171-962 1280). Send for publication catalogue (free).
The FEU is an advisory and intelligence body founded by the Department of Education and Science. It exists to review, lead and support curriculum development and has a policy of inclusion of people who have learning difficulties. A section of the publications catalogue on 'Participation and Equity' includes disabilities and learning difficulties.

The King's Fund Centre, BEBC Ltd., 9 Albion Close, Parkston, Poole, Dorset BH12 3LL (Freephone 0900 262260).
Send for catalogue list of books and videos which relates to all health and social services, including services for people who have learning difficulties. The King's Fund Centre is a health services development agency which promotes improvements in health and social care. This is done by working with those

employed in health services, social services and voluntary agencies and with the users of those services.

BILD (British Institute of Learning Disability), Wolverhampton Rd., Kidderminster, Worcs., DY10 3PP (Tel. 01562 850251).
Send for book list. Other BILD services include:
BILD Bulletin, a collection of articles reproduced from a wide variety of sources on many aspects of learning disability, with a general appeal to anyone working in this area. Published quarterly March, June, Sept, Dec. Sample copies available.
BILD Current Awareness Service (CAS), an extensive bibliography of newly published books and journal articles from Britain, Europe, North America, Australia and New Zealand. It scans over 300 journals each month.
12 issues annually.
Also provides reading lists. A pamphlet gives a list of about 40 headings and for a small fee you can request a reading list on any one topic. This list will include books, teaching aids, resources and journal articles. A literature search will be conducted on any topic not listed at a small cost.

CSV Education in Action.
CSV Education is part of a British national charity, Community Service Volunteers, which creates opportunities for people to play an active part in the life of their community.
Write for publications list to Avanti Books, 8 Parson's Green, Boulton Road, Stevenage, Herts. SG1 4QG.

ALBSU (Adult Literacy and Basic Skills Unit), Kingsbourne House, 229–231 High Holborn, London WC1V 7DA (Tel. 0171-405 4017).
Send for their catalogue and price list. They publish many practical and useful teaching packs, handbooks, readers, videos and films.

The Norah Fry Research Centre, University of Bristol, 32 Tyndall's Park Rd., Bristol BS8 1PY.
A section is given over to research causes of people with learning difficulties.
Send for publications list. Particular emphasis on the transition from hospital to hostel and respite care for families.

Rickitt Educational Media (REM), Educational Software Directory. Ilton, Ilminster, Somerset TA19 9HS (Tel. 01460 57152). Send off for comprehensive catalogue if you have access to a computer.

Other useful British organisations

Citizens' Advice Bureau, National Head Office, 110 Drury Lane, London WC2 5SW.

MENCAP, Royal Society for Mentally Handicapped Children and Adults, 123 Golden Lane, London EC1Y 0RT.

Scottish Society for the Mentally Handicapped, 13 Elmbank Street, Glasgow G2 4QA.

RADAR (Royal Association for Disability and Rehabilitation), 12 City Forum, 250 City Road, London EC1V 8AF.

Mental Handicap in Wales. Applied Research Unit. 44–46 Cowbridge Road East, Cardiff CF1 9DU.

Other useful Irish organisations

National Adult Literacy Agency (NALA), 76 Lower Gardiner Street, Dublin 1, Ireland (Tel. 010 353 1 787205).
NALA has a very good range of literacy and numeracy materials produced in Ireland and overseas. The full range is on display at their Dublin headquarters. They will send out a publication list and prices on request.

The City of Dublin Vocation Education Committee (CDVEC) have a very good Curriculum Development base at: Sundrive Road, Crumlin, Dublin 12, Ireland.
As well as providing a comprehensive reference library for teachers, this unit produces a range of very useful workbook-type programmes for use with adults who have mild learning difficulties. These programmes are practical, age appropriate and provide a very useful resource. They are also very inexpensive.

National Rehabilitation Board Library, 25 Clyde Road, Ballsbridge, Dublin 4, Ireland.
The NRB library has a wide range of books, tapes and materials

on the general topic of rehabilitation with a section especially for people who have learning difficulties. They will send out books and material lists on any subject requested and the library is open to the public.

St Michael's House Library, Child Development and Assessment Clinic, Ballymun, Dublin 9, Ireland (Tel. 010 353 1 375171).
St Michael's House have a small library with a range of books and materials on various aspects of mental handicap.

St Michael's House Research and Development Unit, Lower Kilmacud Road, Stillorgan, Co. Dublin, Ireland (Tel. 010 353 1 288 5805).
Send for publication list and list of useful video material and relevant research projects.

National Association for Mental Handicap in Ireland, 5 Fitzwilliam Place, Dublin 2, Ireland (Tel. 010 353 1 676 6035).
NAMHI have prepared a directory of all mental handicap services in the country. They will send out this booklet on request.

8 Bringing Lifeskills Training To Life

The final chapter of this book will demonstrate, through the use of a Real Life Example, how to put the whole training procedure, as detailed throughout the book, into action. I hope that this example will explain, in a practical way, the sequence of events that the instructor should follow when embarking on Lifeskills training.

The steps in the training procedure are as follows:

STAGE 1: GATHERING INFORMATION
a   Select the trainee(s).
b   Get to know the trainee better—Personal Profile.
c   Identify the trainee's dreams for the future.
d   Using the Lifeskills Network, identify long-, medium- and short-term goals for the trainee.
e   Agree on one skill to begin with.

STAGE 2: PLANNING THE PROGRAMME
a   Complete a task analysis.
b   Identify how much time you have and how it will be used.
c   Invite the trainee(s) to take part in a Training Programme.
d   Liaise with the trainee's family/supervisor.
e   Complete a pre-test.
f   Draw up the timetable, including:
    breaking down the time;
    giving details of each training session;
    indicating location, using a range of teaching methods and materials.
g   Anticipate difficulties which might arise.
h   Sign contract with trainee.

STAGE 3: IMPLEMENTING THE TRAINING PROGRAMME

a   Follow the timetable closely, making sure you:
    use an age-appropriate approach;
    make the maximum use of time;
    prepare sessions carefully;
    use appropriate language;
    are friendly, positive and provide enjoyment;
    deal with problems efficiently and respectfully;
    review progress and adjust timetable where necessary.
b   Evaluate the training programme.
c   Generalise the skill.
d   Make recommendations.

REAL LIFE EXAMPLE OF A LIFESKILLS TRAINING PROGRAMME

STAGE 1: GATHERING INFORMATION

a   Select the trainee

Tim, 28, had worked in a sheltered workshop for the past six years. Individual programme planning meetings, each of which focused on a particular trainee, took place in the workshop on a regular basis. The most recent focused on Tim. It aimed to identify his strengths and needs, and to evaluate how the workshop programme and his home life were utilising his strengths and meeting his needs. This meeting was attended by Tim, his mother and father, his supervisor and the workshop manager.

It was reported at the meeting that Tim was a hard worker who worked slowly but steadily at a particular stage of a production line in the light-assembly unit. The work he did was repetitive but Tim claimed to enjoy it and was not interested in changing his routine.

Tim was an easy-going man, gentle and kind to fellow workers. He was not inclined to initiate conversation but would answer when spoken to and look for assistance when necessary.

When his home situation was discussed, a conflict of interests became evident. Tim claimed, with more conviction in his voice than was evident prior to this, that he had nothing to do at home.

His mother quickly countered this statement, saying, 'Of course you have. He has television, his sound system, plenty of games. You help me in the house and your father in the garden, so you have plenty to do, isn't that right?' Tim, not a man to assert himself, simply said, 'Yes, I suppose so.'

The supervisor, Kate, was anxious that Tim should have the opportunity to express fully what was on his mind and she returned to the point, asking, 'What sort of activities would you like to take part in, in your spare time?'

Tim's voice livened up again. He enjoyed football a lot, he supported Everton and watched every match they played. He also supported a local team but never saw them playing. He knew a fellow on the team and had once been invited to a match but he had not been allowed to go.

His mother interjected, 'Well, you know how rough those football games are, you'd never know what might happen.'

As the meeting progressed it became obvious that Tim was given very little freedom at home. His father seemed to understand Tim's need for more scope to be independent, but his mother was the stronger character and she seemed to have the final say.

The conclusion of the meeting was that Kate should undertake to examine, with Tim, some ways in which he could make more use of his leisure time. Tim's mother agreed to keep an open mind but insisted that no plans would be made without consulting her. This was agreed.

The individual programme planning (IPP) meeting had clearly identified a trainee who needed Lifeskills training.

b   Get to know the trainee better

Kate had been working as a supervisor in the workshop for two years. She thought she knew Tim quite well as a gentle and easy-going person who had much more ability than he was given credit for. He came from a caring family and accepted whatever came his way. The IPP meeting had alerted Kate to the fact that Tim was overprotected at home and that he had needs and frustrations which were not immediately obvious. She knew that she would have to take time really to get to know Tim and decided that the best way was to complete a personal profile.

There were six supervisors in the workshop, five of whom had twelve trainees each to supervise. The sixth was a 'relief' supervisor who assisted the others where necessary. One of the great advantages of having the relief supervisor was that it allowed the others time to work with individuals or small groups within their group of twelve. Kate made arrangements with the relief supervisor to allow her time, over a period of two weeks, to complete a personal profile with Tim. She talked to Tim on a few occasions, visited his home and talked to his parents and, at Tim's request, spoke to his favourite sister, Pat. Kate also sought information from a supervisor who had been employed in the workshop since before Tim started.

Having gathered all this information, Kate now had a much more comprehensive picture of Tim. The process had revealed some very important details, corrected some inaccurate assumptions and confirmed much of what Kate had known already. She arranged the information under headings:

Tim's background

Tim is 28, he was born 8/10/66. He is the youngest of a family of five. He has two brothers and two sisters, each of whom is married, and he has eleven nieces and nephews. Tim has always lived with his parents, in the same house. He went to a special school not far from his home, where he seemed happy but, according to his parents, 'never learnt a thing'. He was always a very gentle, quiet boy, was bullied by others and never made any particular friends. At 18 he went to a vocational training centre. He found it very difficult to settle in and did not like the change in his routine. He played a lot of football there but his mother would not allow him to be in the team as he would have to go to matches at the weekend. The vocational training centre staff identified that Tim was good with his hands and dependable when operating machinery. At 21 he began work in the workshop. It is about six miles from his home. He is friendly with two other trainees but is still inclined to be picked on or bullied by some of the more able and outgoing trainees.

Tim's personality

Tim is a big, strong man physically but his personality is gentle, accepting, non-assertive and shy. He has never had to do anything for himself and, as a result, is dependent and unmotivated. He has very little self-confidence, presuming that he would not be able or would not be allowed to do anything new. Tim does not readily initiate conversation or share thoughts or ideas, and his speech is slow and ponderous. In his mother's company she speaks for him to an alarming extent, not just answering factual information but making decisions on his behalf. For example, if he is asked, 'Where do you like to go at the weekend, Tim?' his mother replies, 'He likes going to his sister's house with his mum and dad. Isn't that right, Tim?'

'Yes,' he answers.

He is a family man not interested in being with other people. Tim is so used to his mother speaking on his behalf that he knows no different and doesn't complain.

Tim has very low self-esteem. He cannot identify anything that he contributes to the life of others, and nothing is expected of him. He has never spoken of any dissatisfaction with his life, but his sister feels that he was never listened to as a child. He grew up thinking that 'it was good to be quiet'. She thinks that 'there is a lot of anger and dissatisfaction under the surface and it needs to be let out'. The opinion at work is that Tim is capable of a great deal more than his lifestyle demands. He has no idea of his own potential and takes no control over his own life or future.

Important people
There are very few important people in Tim's life, mainly because his lifestyle is so restricted.

HIS FATHER. A gentle, loving man, is at home a lot but seems to have very little interaction with his son. He has a rigid routine in his own life and does not like this to be altered. He is peace-loving and quiet and will at all costs avoid a row. The message he most consistently gives to his son is, there's a good lad, do what your mother tells you. During the summer months Tim and his father go fishing. They enjoy this time together.

HIS MOTHER. A loving but domineering woman, has never been able to accept that Tim is an adult with adult needs and interests. She loves her son dearly: 'My life is devoted to Tim and I would do anything for him, I worry that something will happen to him, he can't look after himself.' She treats Tim like a small child, going to great lengths to protect him from any potential danger. This became easier to understand when his mother said, 'I almost lost Tim at birth and then again as a young child, when he ran across a busy road, and a third time as a teenager when he collapsed at a football match. I couldn't cope if it happened again.' Tim says, 'My mum is very good to me. She helps me with everything, she makes lovely dinners and cakes, she stays with me if I can't sleep. Sometimes she won't let me go places but it's for my own good.'

HIS SISTER PAT. 'There are only two years between Tim and me. We were very close as children and played a lot together. It seems as though my life developed from that stage but Tim's life stood still. I get frustrated when I see how little he does for himself, I think he can do much more than he is given credit for.' Pat identified that her mother, with the best will in the world, was the greatest barrier to Tim becoming more independent. She said that Tim takes on a different role altogether in *her* house, helping with the children, washing the dishes, asking for information and giving opinions. Pat has broached the subject of overprotection with her mother but never got very far. Tim's role at home is a well-established pattern now and she can't imagine it ever really changing.

HIS FRIEND TONY. Tony began working in the workshop about two years ago. Their friendship got off to a good start because Kate asked Tim to look after Tony when he came first, show him around and so on, and from that their friendship developed. Tony is a friendly fellow, more outgoing than Tim. He too is inclined to be protective of Tim, tackling others who jeer at him, answering for him and demanding little from him. They do not meet up outside work. At first Tony invited Tim out to several different places but each time Tim replied, 'No, sorry, I'm not allowed', so Tony didn't bother to ask any more. Tim thinks Tony has a great life and would love to be like him: 'He can do whatever he likes.' Tim's mother said that he could invite Tony over for tea whenever he wanted but Tim didn't want to invite him. He didn't want Tony to see him being treated like a baby at home.

Lifestyle

Tim's lifestyle is very limited indeed and there is no real reason
for this. He suffers from epilepsy but this is well controlled with
daily medication. He is very responsible about taking his tablets
at work and his mother gives them to him at home. He has not
had an epileptic seizure for over four years now; however, his
epilepsy is another major concern for his mother. There are very
few places where Tim goes without his mother. One is work, to
which he travels on a special bus which picks him up at his door,
and the other is Pat's house. She collects him every second
Sunday and brings him to her house for the day. Other than these
and some family outings, he spends all his time at home.

He uses no community facilities even though he lives in a very
central location, close to many amenities. He is not able to use
public transport and has never tried. Pat suggested to her mother
that she should encourage Tim to go to the local shop for a simple
message. Her mother replied, 'But why would I bother him,
can't I do it more quickly myself?' At home Tim watches
television every evening after his dinner and goes to bed at 9.30.
On Saturday he has a bath, goes to the shop with his father for
the paper and his magazines and watches football on television.
On Sunday he goes to church with his parents and sometimes for
a drive or outing afterwards. Every second Sunday he goes to
Pat's house.

Tim loves football. He used to play a lot as a child but he is too
heavy now and his mum says it wouldn't be good for him to run
around. He supports Everton football team; he watches all their
matches and most other important matches. He collects pictures
of his team which he cuts out of football magazines. He also
supports a local team, for which his neighbour plays. He would
love to be able to go to local football matches.

Tim hates rows and fights, they frighten him. As a result he
does not argue with his mother or defend himself if he is picked
on at work. If he feels very cross or upset he goes to his bedroom
and plays a tape.

Tim has a lot of money saved, as his mother puts all his wages
into the post office for him. He is not allowed to carry money; his
mum says, 'He has no need of money, it would only make him
more vulnerable.'

Role in life

At home Tim's primary role is that of a child: decisions are made for him, everything is done for him, nothing is demanded of him. He lives a comfortable, completely routine life, in the care of his parents.

At work he has a more independent and important role. He is a respected and dependable worker who operates stage 3 in the assembly line without any assistance. He can identify problems and bring them to the attention of the supervisor.

He is a good friend to Tony, helping him out where possible, he is caring and generous. In general, Tim gets on well with his fellow workers but by some he is seen as an easy target for jeering and picking on because he does not retaliate or get others into trouble.

Tim has very few opportunities in his life to make choices; as a result, when such opportunities arise, he is unsure what to do. He was asked if he would like to take part in a keep-fit class at work. 'I don't know,' he replied, 'I'll ask my mother.'

Over the years he has been in the workshop the staff have developed an image of Tim as 'a gentle giant', quiet, methodical and slow-moving, 'an epileptic' who is afraid to go out alone. Very overprotected at home, not worth teaching him Lifeskills, he won't be allowed to use them. Very little to say for himself but seems happy.

Kate did not accept this summary. She had always thought that there was a lot more to Tim than met the eye. Having supervised his work for two years, setting new targets and introducing new skills, she had observed a lot of developments that would not have been thought possible. She thought that Tim's self-esteem and respect were very low and that the atmosphere in his home was disempowering. He had very little awareness of his own potential and, therefore, no motivation to change his lifestyle. His fear of conflict and anger prevented him from challenging his mother's decisions and opinions. Kate then summarised Tim's needs:

Needs

First and foremost Tim needs to learn that he can and should have a lot more control over his own life. He needs to be reassured that this can be a gradual process which, if handled with care, will not upset or anger his mother. Tim needs to take on the responsibility to 'teach' his mother that he is an adult, with adult needs. Before trying to change his mother, he must change himself, believe in himself. Tim thought he would not be able to manage the complicated stage 3 of the assembly line and said he was happy to remain at the less demanding job he had been doing for three years. With a little pressure and lots of encouragement he gave it a try. No one was more surprised than himself when he mastered the task without any difficulty.

The greatest obstacle to Tim taking more control of his own life and future is the attitude and fears of his mother and the rigid pattern of his home life. This life-long pattern will not be changed overnight, nor his mother's concerns easily dealt with. It will be a slow process but it is long overdue. Tim's mother will need to be given great support in giving Tim more freedom. Her worries must be respected and her love and good intentions acknowledged.

Neither Tim nor his mother could cope with too much change too quickly. Tim will have to take control of his life a little bit at a time, becoming confident at each step before taking on anything new. Tim needs to demonstrate his capability to his mother, gradually winning her confidence in his ability to manage. He will have to stand up for himself and his wishes for the future and realise that this sort of self-assertion need not lead to rows or anger.

Tim needs to identify the most important changes that he would like to make and decide which would be the best to start off with:

1   To go to the local football matches.
2   To play in the football team at work.
3   To travel to work independently.
4   To take my own tablets at home.
5   To decide when I want to have a shower or a bath.
6   To choose my own clothes.
7   To join a club and attend it on one or two evenings a week.
8   To make my own way to Pat's house.
9   To meet Tony at the weekend.
10 To stand up for myself at work.

SUMMARISE PERSONAL PROFILE. Kate and Tim summarised Tim's personal profile for easy reference, on a personal profile poster.

PERSONAL PROFILE POSTER

Date: 6-4-'94

Personality

Gentle
Pleasant ☺
Non-assertive
Dependant 👥
Un-motivated
low self-esteem
lots of hidden
        potential 🚪
loves football ⚽

Background

Tim is 28
the youngest of 5
All other family
    members married
lives at home with
    parents
Very over-protected
Not much good
    at school
Works in a
Sheltered work-
shop

Important People

Mother
Father
Pat (sister)
Tony (friend at work)
Kate (supervisor)
other family members

Focus Person

Name: Tim

Date of birth: 8-10-'66

Its my life and
its up to me to
make the best of it.

Lifestyle

Very limited
Home / work / Pat's house
Not allowed out
Does nothing for himself
Watches T.V.
Special bus to work
No social life

Role in Life

child
victim
No choices
Accepting
dependable worker
    brother
    friend.

Needs

To take control
To go to football
        matches
To go out and about
To help my mother
to see that I am
an adult.

To make choices

To stand up for
    myself

c   Identify the trainee's dream for the future

Going through the process of drawing up his own personal
profile with Kate was the first time Tim had ever really looked at
his own life. At many stages during this process, he compared
himself and his lifestyle with other people. Up to now Tim had
been happy enough with his life—or was he simply resigned to it
in a helpless sort of way? Completing the personal profile and
looking at all aspects of his life had the effect of making him quite
dissatisfied. Kate was glad to see this: he had had good reason to
be dissatisfied and dissatisfaction is a great motivator of change.

This new sense of dissatisfaction was a great help when Kate
asked Tim to think about his future, to express his wishes and
desires. She asked him to describe the lifestyle that he would like
to have. After almost every wish that Tim expressed he added,
'But I won't be allowed.' Kate had to keep reminding him that
dreaming was planning ahead with all barriers and obstacles
removed. She wanted him really to let himself go, to express
wishes for the future that he had never been allowed to express
and identify things that he wanted to change.

Tim's dreams began to unfold, with the help of some con-
structive questions from Kate:

> Where will you live?
> Where will you work?
> What will you do in the evenings and at weekends?
> What will you do for yourself?
> What will you spend your money on?

The future which Tim described was totally different from his
current lifestyle. As it unfolded it began to gain momentum and
became more enthusiastic and 'daring'. Kate listened inter-
estedly to all that he had to say, noting the main points. The fact
that she accepted what he was saying, imposed no limitation and
praised and encouraged his thoughts and ideas, helped the
dreaming process.

Tim's dreams for the future provided ample material to make
plans for Lifeskills training that would help him to develop in the
direction in which he wanted to go. Among his thoughts were:

> I want to be able to say I'm going out to . . . and I'll be back by
> 11 o'clock.

I want to go to the local football matches with Steve next door.

I'd love to be able to stand up to my mum.

I'd love to do something for my mum instead of her doing everything for me.

I want to go in a bus and a train and even walk to places on my own—I love my mum but I'm too big to have her beside me all the time.

I'm going to have a smart answer for Billy when he calls me names.

I'd love to score for Everton.

I'd like to live with Pat when my parents get too old or sick to manage, but first I'm going to show them what I can do for myself, then they won't have to worry any more.

I'd like to have more friends.

I'd like to work in a real factory.

I want to decide small things for myself—what I will wear, when I will shave and wash, what I'll have for supper, etc.

Not all Tim's dreams were realistic, but they gave a very clear picture of the sort of future he was starting to build for himself.

Kate suggested that they concentrate on establishing a life outside the home, using community facilities, going places, using public transport, joining in community activities. Alongside this would have to be assertiveness—saying what he wanted to do, within reason, and showing his mother that he was well capable of doing it. Tim agreed.

d   Using the Lifeskills Network, identify, long- medium- and short-term goals for the trainee

Having agreed on their main target area, Tim and Kate drew up a *long-term goal* (see Chapter 3):

In one year's time, Tim will, with his parents' approval, travel to work independently. He will play for the football team at work and attend the home matches of his local football club, when he chooses.

This long-term goal pointed them in the direction of the core skill 'community skills' in the Lifeskills Network (see Chapter 1). They examined the six main skill areas and agreed that three of these related directly to the long-term goal.

1   Use of public transport.
2   Using your community.
3   Safety in the community.

They decided to work on the public transport and related safety skills first and they drew up a *medium-term goal*:

> In six months' time, Tim will travel independently on public transport to and from work. He will cross the road safely using the correct method. He will be familiar with selected landmarks and be able to ask for assistance. He will use a public telephone in case of emergency.

The ability to use public transport would really transform Tim's life and he was quite excited at the prospect. However, he kept referring back to his mother: 'She'll never let me, I know she'll never let me.' Kate accepted his concerns and knew that they were well-founded. She reminded him that they were planning over a period of six months and that they would take one small step at a time. They would seek his parents' approval in small steps also, so that his mother and father would gradually accept Tim's need and ability to become more independent.

They consulted the Lifeskills Network again, examining the individual tasks under the main skill 'use of public transport'. The first individual task under this heading was 'road safety skills'. Tim had not been allowed to go out alone, let alone cross a road alone, since he was almost knocked down by a car when he was nine years old. He would have to become confident at this task before he could go any further. They agreed on a *short-term goal*:

> In three months' time, Tim will walk safely along the footpath. He will cross the pedestrian crossings adjacent to his home and his work, confidently and using the correct method. He will practise this skill each day while he works towards the goal of using public transport independently.

e   Agree on one skill to begin with

The skill which Tim and Kate agreed to work on in order to achieve Tim's short-term goal was 'using a pedestrian crossing'.

STAGE 2:   PLANNING THE TRAINING PROGRAMME

a   Complete a task analysis

Kate organised with the relief supervisor to have one morning
and one afternoon per week to work with Tim. She sought
permission from the workshop manager and checked to ensure
that this arrangement would not clash with any other staff or
trainee activities. Initially she would use this time to prepare the
training programme. The first step in her preparation was to
ensure that she knew every detail of the skill herself. She sat
down to complete a task analysis (see Chapter 4). She imagined

herself using a pedestrian crossing and listed each action involved. She thought that she had included everything but decided to check out the accuracy of the task analysis by putting it into action. She went to use the pedestrian crossing near the workshop as though she had never used it before. She followed her own task analysis to guide her through each action. She was amazed to find that she had left out several important points, included some unnecessary details, and put some of the actions in the wrong order. She noted all the necessary changes as she completed the task. Having rewritten the task analysis she put it into practice once more. This time it guided her smoothly through the whole process and she was satisfied that it was logical and comprehensive.

Task analysis for using a pedestrian crossing
- Identify the colour red.
- Identify the colour green.
- Associate red with wait.
- Associate green with cross.
- Know what a pedestrian crossing looks like.
- Understand what a pedestrian crossing is for.
- Identify types of traffic which use the road.
- Understand the dangers of careless crossing.
- Know the direction in which to walk.
- Walk safely along footpath.
- Locate the pedestrian crossing.
- Stand beside the crossing.
- Locate the button to signal wish to cross.
- Locate pedestrian lights opposite.
- Press the button.
- Identify red/green light in the shape of a man standing/walking.
- Interpret standing 'red man' to mean wait.
- Wait while 'red man' is lighting.
- Keep looking at signal opposite.
- Observe when 'green man' lights up.
- Interpret walking 'green man' to mean 'cross.'
- Check to ensure that all traffic has stopped.
- Walk straight across the road without delay.
- Know the direction in which to walk on the far side.

b   Identify how much time you have and how it will be used

Each supervisor was allowed to devote one day per week to
Lifeskills training with an individual or a small group. Kate
decided that it would be best to split up the day, working for a
morning early in the week and an afternoon later in the week. A
full day might be too tiring or demanding of Tim's concentration.
Tuesday morning and Thursday afternoon would suit her. She
checked these times with the relief supervisor and would check
them with Tim when they met to discuss the training programme. She had chosen a morning and afternoon so that they
would be able to use the pedestrian crossing at the times when
Tim would use it while travelling to and from work. She would
take three weeks (one morning and one afternoon per week) to
prepare the programme and eight weeks to implement the
programme. A further two weeks would be required to evaluate
the programme, generalise the skill and make recommendations.

c   Invite the trainee to take part in a training programme

Kate arranged to have a meeting with Tim on a Thursday
afternoon at 2 p.m., a mutually suitable time. This meeting was
to outline the training plans which she had prepared to work on
the agreed skill and help Tim to reach his short-term goal.
   The meeting started promptly and Kate outlined:

- What the training programme would involve (with reference
  to the task analysis).
- How long it would take in her estimation—eight weeks, two
  half-days per week.
- The days and times that suited her, checking to see if they
  suited him.
- Where the training programme would be located—room A
  in the workshop and in the community.
- What the objective would be and how this related to Tim's
  medium- and long-term goals.

Kate asked Tim what he thought of all this and encouraged him
to ask questions if there was anything which he wasn't sure
about. Tim's initial reaction was, 'But I thought I would be
learning how to go on the bus.' Kate explained how this skill

related to his long-term goal and how important it was to be safe and to assure his mother of his road safety skills, before going any further. Once this was explained, Tim was interested and enthusiastic about the training programme. He could understand how necessary it was to be able to cross the road safely in order to travel independently by bus, but he had two problems:

- He had a PE class on a Tuesday morning.
- He did not feel able to talk to his mother about the training programme. He was afraid that she would not allow it and that he wouldn't be able to tell her how important it was.

Kate asked if Monday morning would suit him better. Tim said that would be fine and Kate agreed to discuss it with the relief supervisor.

Kate asked if Tim would like her to come to his house so that they could discuss the matter with his mother together. He thought that this was a great idea. She suggested going to his house the following Monday morning; they could return to work together after the meeting. Tim said that he would check this out with his parents.

d   Liaise with the trainee's family

Kate confirmed the arrangement to go to Tim's house on the Monday morning and agreed to be there at 10 o'clock. Knowing of Tim's mother's worries and reluctance to allow him to go out alone, she knew that this idea would have to be 'sold' very carefully.

Kate began the meeting by talking about other family members, how life had been when they were all small, how the parents had felt when they started to become independent and go out alone. She asked if the parents could recall any particular worries and concerns around that time. Tim's mother related a range of interesting and funny stories recalling many worries which she had had over the years. Kate told some incidents that had happened in her life also; these were similar and, they all agreed, just part of growing up.

Kate asked Tim's mother what would have been the reaction if she had refused any of her other children permission to go out alone. 'Once they were over 18,' she replied, 'they went whether

I approved or not!' Kate explained how important it was for Tim to experience the same sort of freedom, to a certain degree. Because he was not an assertive sort of person he had not insisted on becoming independent, but that was not a reflection on his wish or need to do so. Kate stated gently, but in no uncertain terms, 'Unless Tim learns gradually to become more independent of you, he will find it very difficult to cope in the future when you are not there to help him.'

Tim's mother could see that Kate was making sense, but she couldn't get out of her mind the fright and worry that she had experienced when he ran across the road as a child,

Kate said that that was exactly what they hoped to deal with: Tim needed to learn how to cross the road safely and confidently, otherwise the worry of him being knocked down would haunt his mother for the rest of her life!

'I need to learn, Mum, I want to do it by myself'. His father said, 'The lad has a point.'

Kate assured Tim's parents that she would carefully supervise every stage of the programme. They agreed that when she and Tim were satisfied that the skill had been mastered, they would come and give a demonstration, so that his parents could see for themselves how well he could manage.

They agreed to allow Tim to take part in the training programme. Kate had a simple form prepared which she asked them to sign, officially giving their permission for Tim to take part in the programme. This was important from the point of view of 1) ensuring that everything was above board in the unlikely event of an accident, and 2) ensuring that the parents would not change their minds halfway through without an acceptable reason for doing so.

Tim hugged his mother, delighted and amazed at the outcome of the meeting. 'This could be the start of the new me,' he said excitedly.

e Complete the pre-test

Kate drew up a checklist from the task analysis and went through each stage of the process with Tim to establish what he could do and what he had difficulty with:

CHECKLIST		
Skill: Using a Pedestrian Crossing		
Name: Tim		
	Pre-Test	Post-Test
Can identify the colour red	√	
Can identify the colour green	0	
Can associate red with wait	0	
Can associate green with cross	0	
Knows what a pedestrian crossing looks like	0	
Can understand what a pedestrian crossing is for	0	
Can identify five types of traffic that use the road	(3)	
Can understand the dangers of careless crossing	0	
Knows the direction in which to walk	0	
Can walk safely along the footpath	√	
Can locate the pedestrian crossing	0	
Can stand beside the crossing	0	
Can locate the button to signal wish to cross	0	
Can locate pedestrian lights opposite	0	
Knows to press the button	0	
Can interpret 'standing red man' to mean wait	0	
Can wait while 'red man' is lighting	0	
Can concentrate on the signal opposite	0	
Can observe when the 'green man' lights up	0	
Can interpret a 'walking green man' to mean cross	0	
Can check to ensure that all traffic has stopped	0	
Can walk straight across the road without delay	0	
Knows the direction in which to walk on the far side	0	
Test(s) completed	18/4/94	

f Draw up a timetable

	TIMETABLE FOR 8-WEEK TRAINING PROGRAMME	
Skill:	Using a Pedestrian Crossing	
Name:	Tim	
Dates:	Starting: 25.4.94　　　　Finishing: 17.6.94.	
	Monday 9 a.m.–1 p.m.	**Thursday 2 p.m.–4.30 p.m.**
Wk 1	**Location: Training Room** ● Identify the colour green, talk about things that are always green—grass, trees. ● Paint a picture using green only. ● Find six green objects: —in the room; —outside (15 min. walk). ● Play matching games, using cards of four colours. ● From a range of colours pick the green.	**Location: Training Room** ● Recap previous session. ● Identify green and red. ● Pick green and red out from several different colours and name both. ● Associate red with WAIT and green with CROSS. ● Using two coloured light bulbs Tim has to shout out wait or cross as the bulb lights up.
Wk 2	**Location: Training Room and Work Crossing** ● Identify a pedestrian crossing from a photograph. ● Examine and name each different part of the crossing. ● Make a pedestrian crossing poster, which illustrates the main aspects of the crossing. ● Find crossing closest to workshop and name different parts.	**Location: Training Room** ● Discuss traffic. ● Ask Tim to name all the types of vehicle he knows. ● Divide these into categories. ● Discuss how each one uses the road and the danger it can cause. ● Make a traffic poster, cut cars and other vehicles from magazines and stick them onto a 'street', which was painted onto a poster.

	TIMETABLE continued SKILL—Using a Pedestrian Crossing	
	Monday 9 a.m.–1 p.m.	**Thursday 2 p.m.–4.30 p.m.**
Wk 3	**Location: Training Room and Work Crossing** • What can happen if a person is careless crossing the road?—Discussion. • Give examples—hospital, broken bones, upset caused, etc. • Worksheet—careless behaviour leads to . . . (illustrations of possible outcomes). • Go out of the workshop. • Tim has to locate nearest crossing, walking safely along the footpath.	**Location: Training Room** • Recap. • Show slides 'Take Care of Yourself', the section on road safety. Discuss what the person is doing wrong and see the consequences. • Remember the safety steps given on the slides—Kate write them down. • Role-play—a friend misbehaving while crossing the road, how to react.
Wk 4	**Location: Training Room and Work Crossing** • To recap—look at and discuss the road safety slides. • Take out pedestrian crossing poster. Identify all the parts, button signal, lights opposite, etc. • Go out to pedestrian lights, name and point out all important parts. • Watch Kate as she uses the pedestrian crossing. • Go through the process together. • Repeat.	**Location: Training Room** • Recap on using the pedestrian crossing. Did Tim notice anything in particular? • Play a game to improve observation skills—a series of cards, some blank, some with a green man, some with a red man. • Kate deals them out, Tim has to watch carefully and call out green—cross, or red—wait, as the green and red man are shown up. • Role-play—losing your way.

	TIMETABLE continued SKILL—Using a Pedestrian Crossing	
	Monday 9 a.m.–1 p.m.	Thursday 2 p.m.–4.30 p.m.
Wk 5	**Location: Training Room and Work Crossing** • Recap on the different parts of the pedestrian crossing. • Play observation 'green and red man' game once more. • Go out to the crossing. • Tim goes through the process following Kate's instructions. • Role-play—if others do not use the pedestrian crossing properly.	**Location: Training Room and Work Crossing** • In order to ensure that Tim notices the traffic and potential dangers. Play observation game 'First to spot a bus, motorbike, taxi, ambulance, etc.' • Ask Tim to locate pedestrian crossing. • Ask him to give the steps, confirm or correct his instruction. • Carry out each step together.
Wk 6	**Location: Training Room and Work Crossing** • Watch set of road safety slides again which point out correct method and potential dangers. • Go to the pedestrian crossing. • Kate crosses first and waits on the other side. • Tim crosses independently over to her. • Repeat several times. • Travel in Kate's car to see how a motorist observes the pedestrian code.	**Location: Training Room and Work Crossing** • Discuss ways of checking to ensure that traffic stops, looking in each direction. First right then left. • Go to the pedestrian crossing. • Kate stands by Tim as he performs the skills but gives no verbal instructions. • Repeat several times. • Complete worksheet on using the crossing safely.

	Monday 9 a.m.–1 p.m.	Thursday 2 p.m.–4.30 p.m.
	TIMETABLE continued **SKILL—Using a Pedestrian Crossing**	
Wk 7	**Location: Tim's Local Crossing** • Go to Tim's house. • Use the crossing adjacent to work. • When on the other side, which direction is it to the bus to get to Tim's house? • Tim to cross on his own, travel together to Tim's house by bus, locate crossing closest to Tim's house. • Note any differences between them.	**Location: Tim's Local Crossing** • Recap on any differences between the crossing at Tim's house and the one at work. • Travel to Tim's house by bus. • Practise using the pedestrian crossing closest to his house. Firstly accompany him, then observe at a distance. • Invite Tim's parents to see how well he can manage.
Wk 8	**Location: Training Room and Work Crossing** • Tim gives Kate a training session on traffic, road safety, pedestrian crossings, correct behaviour, etc. • He brings Kate to the crossing as though she had never seen it before. • Instruct her in each step of how to cross. Complete the procedure without any assistance himself. • Make a personal identity card.	**Location: Training Room and Coffee Shop** • Evalute training programme. Did it achieve the goals it set out to achieve? If so, congratulate Tim. • To celebrate what has been achieved, cross the road to the coffee shop and enjoy tea or coffee and a cake together. • Discuss next step towards Tim's long-term goal.

g   Anticipate difficulties which might arise

Having completed the timetable, Kate tried to anticipate any difficulties which might occur in the course of the training programme and make plans to avoid them.

1   Her main concern was that Tim's mother would change her mind and try to put a stop to the training programme. She thought that Tim's mother, with her anxiety about the situation, would be looking for reasons to find fault with the programme. Kate would have to take every precaution to

ensure that nothing went wrong. By asking Tim's parents to sign an agreement, they had made some commitment to the running and completion of the training programme; this might help to prevent them changing their minds.

Kate decided that she would link up frequently with Tim's parents, giving them positive feedback about any progress which Tim made. This would give them encouragement and they in turn could acknowledge Tim's achievements.

2   Kate was not sure about the speed at which Tim would progress. She had not done any Lifeskills training with him before and could only allocate time to learn each element of the skill, based on how he performed at work. She prepared a series of useful and relevant worksheets which she could use if a training session was completed more quickly than expected. In the event of the training process taking longer than anticipated, she had organised a review date in the middle to check progress and make alterations if necessary.

3   If bad weather made it impossible to go out and use the pedestrian crossing, Kate planned to swap sessions on the timetable which was mixed between indoor and outdoor work.

4   It was possible that the pedestrian crossing closest to Tim's house would be slightly different from the one near work. Although most of the training would be carried out on the crossing near work, Kate had included a visit to Tim's house to inform his parents of progress to date. This visit would include time to identify any differences between the crossings and then to practise using Tim's local crossing.

5   Because of Tim's low self-esteem, Kate was concerned that he might lose heart or give up if progress, at any stage, was slower than he expected. In order to keep his motivation up as much as possible, she had set realistic mini-goals. She aimed to acknowledge, at the end of each training session, something positive which had been achieved, even if it fell short of the goal which was set. She would recap often on what had been achieved to date and give regular and realistic praise.

She would encourage Tim to express his thoughts on, and reactions to, the training programme at regular intervals so that negative feelings would be less likely to build up unknown to her.

TRAINING PROGRAMME

CONTRACT

Title of Training Programme: Using a Pedestrian crossing

Dates: From: 25.4.94   To: 17.6.94

Times: From: - 9.30 am   To: 1.00 pm (MON)
and - 2.00 pm   4 30 pm (THURS)

Location: Training room in workshop and real
situation.

Objectives:

1. Tim will know the colours red and green
2. Tim will walk safely along the
footpath.
3. Tim will use the pedestrian crossing
adjacent to his work and home.
4.

Specific Rules/Requirements: Written permission from Tim's parents.

Tim will speak about his reactions /
concerns.

Tim will organise to have daily
practice at this skill

On this Training Programme I will train/learn to the best of my ability. I will stick to the
rules that we have agreed. I will make every effort to reach the goal that we have set . I
will attend regularly and on time and when this is not possible I will inform the other party in
advance.

Signed

Date: 22-4-94   **Trainee:** Tim   **Instructor:** Kate

I have completed or wish to leave this Training Programme and understand that if I leave I
cannot re-join.

Date: **Signed:**

h   Sign a contract with the trainee

Kate outlined the details and objectives of the training programme on a simple form. She arranged to meet Tim at an
agreed time a few days before the training programme was due
to begin. Together they went through the contract, confirming
starting dates, times, objectives and requirements. When both
parties understood exactly what was required of them and were
satisfied with all the details, they each signed the form.

STAGE 3: IMPLEMENTING THE TRAINING PROGRAMME

a   Follow the timetable closely

Kate had spent a lot of time preparing the timetable. She had
worked directly from the task analysis, ensuring that every
element of the skill would be covered in the training programme.
She went through the timetable with Tim, explaining the relevance of each session. Tim was very pleased to see that Kate had
incorporated the suggestions which he had made at their first
meeting. Having invested this time and effort, and completed a
timetable with which both parties were satisfied, it was obvious
that they should follow it closely.

Their decision to adhere to the timetable was tested at times—
for example, Tim came into the fourth training session in tears.
He was upset because some of the other trainees were taunting
him. They called him a baby because he couldn't cross the road
by himself. They asked him if Kate was his new girlfriend and
said that they would tell his mother. Instead of standing up for
himself or laughing back at them, Tim started to cry. Of course,
this only made the taunting worse.

Kate was very tempted to deviate from the timetable to
include some training in assertiveness. Although this training
was badly needed, the timing would not have been right and the
assertiveness training would not have been properly prepared.
Kate realised that including extra sessions such as this, no matter
how necessary, would cause confusion and reduce the likelihood
of reaching the original goal on time. Instead, she took note of
this need so that it could be addressed at the planning stage of
Tim's next training programme.

Early on in the training programme, Tim had real difficulty identifying the colour green. Kate was concerned that he might be colour blind and offered to arrange an eye test for him. This had not been planned and it took up a whole training session. However, it was essential that this matter be investigated if the programme was to go ahead. The optician reported that Tim appeared to have great difficulty identifying colours but that there was no medical reason for this. He suggested that Kate should concentrate on using the green and red bulbs as teaching aids. The light would show up the colour most clearly and also relate closely to how the colours would be seen at the pedestrian crossing.

Eventually, the two colours and their associated instructions 'wait' and 'cross' were indelibly imprinted on Tim's mind. 'I'll know those two colours till the day I die,' he said, delighted with himself.

The training programme was now running three sessions behind the timetable. Kate hoped that they might make up some time in the following sessions. She thought it likely that Tim would understand the crossing procedure quite quickly. In any case, they had agreed a review date at the end of the fourth week, at which time they would check progress and alter the timetable if necessary.

While following the timetable closely, Kate kept a series of important points in mind. She was careful to:

Use an age-appropriate approach

As a result of his over-protective home situation, Tim was inclined to be quite childish at times. Kate was therefore particularly anxious to use an age-appropriate approach. She decided to make the best possible use of this one-to-one situation with Tim, aiming to increase his self-confidence and self-respect. She did this by showing her respect for him in every possible way—seeking his opinions, using his ideas, acknowledging his ability and accepting him for who he was.

She was open about identifying her own weaknesses and used every opportunity to emphasise that they were working together—it was not a case of her leading and him following. She made it clear that she expected adult behaviour and communication from him and explained that if he developed this more adult behaviour, he would probably be more respected by others.

Make the maximum use of time

Kate did not have a great reputation for punctuality. She admitted this openly to Tim and said that she would make a special effort during the training programme. Tim, on the other hand, was an excellent time-keeper and was always ready for an appointment five or ten minutes in advance. He gave Kate a tip: 'If you want to be somewhere on time, tell yourself that the deadline is ten minutes before it actually is—then you'll always have a few minutes to spare.' Kate said that sounded like a good idea. She would put it into practice and let him know how it worked.

In the course of the training programme she was late on only two occasions, once following an accident in her workroom, and the second time because she missed her bus to work. On both occasions she apologised to Tim who was, as always, pleasant and accepting.

Kate took steps to ensure there were as few interruptions as possible. She informed the workshop manager and staff of the times and location of the training programme. She asked, if possible, that they would not be interrupted except in the case of an emergency. She also asked the secretary to tell callers that she and Tim were unavailable and to take messages unless calls were urgent.

Prepare sessions carefully

Kate found that the easiest way to ensure that each training session was well prepared, was to write 'session notes'. She kept a small notebook for this purpose. The session notes contained such information as:

- Objective of the session.
- Allocation of time within session.
- Equipment and materials required.
- Points to look out for or emphasise.

Kate's session notes for the first training session on the timetable looked like this:

Objective
That Tim could dependably identify the colour green.

Time
Complete first three activities before the tea break and the other three between break and lunch.

Equipment needed
At least six green objects.
Some magazines, scissors and glue.
Two large sheets of plain paper.
Green paint, paint brush and jar of water.
Colour-matching game.
Set of colour cards.

NB
Check carefully that he knows the colour—it seems to pose
problems for him.

Kate usually took a few minutes the day before a training session
to gather the necessary equipment and read over the notes. As a
result the training sessions ran very smoothly.

Use appropriate language
Tim's verbal skills were very good and he had no difficulty
understanding Kate's instructions. However, Kate built in a
checking mechanism to ensure that all instructions were understood. Whenever she introduced a new word, for example, when
identifying the parts of a pedestrian crossing, she would check
back each word with him saying, 'Now you tell me the name of
each part.' At the end of each session she asked Tim to practise the
part of the skill which they had just learnt by teaching it to her.
This gave her a clear indication of how much he had understood.

    In order to ensure that she gave the same instructions each
time Tim used the pedestrian crossing, Kate wrote out the
sequence of actions in clear, concise sentences. By following
these each time she instructed Tim, she knew that she would not
confuse him by making changes.

Be friendly, positive and provide enjoyment
Kate ensured that the atmosphere of the training programme
was warm and friendly. She did this by making it clear that she
was Tim's equal and not in a position of authority. She always
made sure that there was a little time for chatting at the start of
the training session. She tried each day to have some news or
information to share with Tim and listened attentively to whatever he had to say.

Throughout the preparation and implementation of the training programme Kate focused on what Tim *could* do and what further achievements she hoped he would make by the end of each session and the whole programme. In Tim's home there was a lot of emphasis on what he was *not* able to do, and would *never* be able to do. The result was low self-confidence leading to reduced effort and motivation and therefore few achievements. Kate knew that to build up Tim's self-confidence would be a slow process, but she was going to ensure that this training programme at least started that process.

When drawing up the timetable, she was aware of the need for light relief, variety and real enjoyment. She included some activities which she knew would particularly appeal to Tim. She hoped to demonstrate the value of being able to laugh at yourself. 'If you are able to laugh at yourself, Tim, you will find that others laugh with you and not at you.' They enjoyed several amusing incidents in the course of the programme; the best one was when Tim was standing at the pedestrian crossing one day waiting for the 'green man' to appear. A little old lady tapped him on the shoulder and asked him to help her across. Tim said that he would be delighted and was very pleased to be asked. When he had brought the woman safely across, she said, 'Ah, if only I was about fifty years younger, you could have made me a great husband!'

Deal with problems efficiently and respectfully

Three problems arose during the training programme and Kate dealt with them so efficiently that they were overcome without loss of pride, disappointment or upset.

The first was Tim's difficulty in identifying the colour green and associating it with the instruction to cross. This was overcome by visiting the optician who gave some useful advice and removed concern about Tim's sight. Also, by calmly allowing more time to concentrate on the colour green, Tim was allowed, without feeling rushed or embarrassed, to acquire this aspect of the skill, with confidence.

'I've got it, Kate, I've got it!' He was so pleased with himself. 'I know I've wasted two of our training sessions but I couldn't help it.'

'Indeed you haven't wasted sessions,' Kate replied. 'You have put them to excellent use—without being sure of those colours we could not have proceeded with the training programme. Well done, Tim, I'm delighted with you!'

Because of the visit to the optician and the two extra sessions working on the colour green and what it indicated, Kate was aware that they were now three sessions behind the timetable. She was wondering about extending the course but was not sure how much longer they would need. She decided instead that she would wait until the date came for them to review the timetable—at the end of the fourth week. She hoped that Tim might make up time while doing other aspects of the programme.

The third problem in the course of the training programme was some further concerns which his mother expressed in relation to the new skill. One day Tim and Kate were practising at the crossing when suddenly it started to rain very heavily. Although they returned immediately to the workshop, both of them were very wet. Tim's coat did not dry during the remainder of the afternoon. When he arrived home with his coat still wet through, his mother said, 'This training will have to stop.' Tim was really disappointed. 'Ah, please, Mum, it's going great.' Kate spoke to Tim's mother, explaining how, with unpredictable weather, it was impossible to organise dry days for training sessions. However, she thought that Tim had handled the situation very well, making it back to the workshop as quickly as possible. Kate suggested that a new or a different coat would be a considerable help in overcoming this problem. The light jacket that he normally wore would not keep out the rain at all.

Not only did Kate persuade Tim's mother to allow him to stay on the course, he got a new coat, too!

Review progress and adjust the timetable where necessary
Progress at the start of the training programme was much slower than either Kate or Tim had expected. Tim was getting frustrated with the repetitive work on identifying the colour green and understanding what it indicated. Kate could see that there was *some* progress and she used every opportunity to convey this to Tim, because she knew it was difficult for him to keep up the effort. Each day she did several tests using the green and red bulbs. She flashed one colour bulb on, asking Tim what colour it

was and what instruction it gave. She repeated this ten times, changing the colour randomly, and noting how many times he got the colour and the instruction right. The number of correct answers increased slowly but surely and by day four of the programme, Tim was consistently responding correctly ten times out of ten. At one point Kate had wondered if she should persist with this aspect of the skill or move on to something new in order to give them both a break, with the intention of returning to it later. However, when she examined the rest of the timetable she realised that it would be impossible to go any further without a clear understanding of the colours red and green, and what they both indicated on the pedestrian crossing.

Once Tim became confident of the colours, the training programme really took off. His observation skills were very good and he was quick to follow the procedure of using the pedestrian crossing. He retained information very well and did not require all the repetition which Kate had incorporated into the timetable. By the agreed review date they had comfortably made up for lost time and were on target. In fact, Tim was progressing so quickly now that they agreed to include an extra aspect of the skill in place of some repetition which now seemed unnecessary. On the Thursday of week seven they decided to go to the pedestrian crossing which he would have to use when attending a local football match. It differed slightly from the other two, as it was situated at a more complex junction. However, Tim mastered it without difficulty. This was very important to him and really made him feel that he was 'getting places'.

b Evaluate the training programme

The skill of 'using a pedestrian crossing' is concrete and easy to measure. The trainee can be observed performing the skill and the checklist marked appropriately as he goes through each stage. The first time that Tim completed the skill correctly he was delighted with himself and he and Kate fully acknowledged this achievement. Tim then thought that they should move on to the next goal. Kate encouraged him not to rush ahead, explaining that to complete a skill correctly once was not enough evidence to suggest that he was completely competent at it. This point was demonstrated by the fact that the next time Tim went through the procedure he omitted two important steps. He did not concentrate on the signal opposite and therefore did not notice immediately when the 'green man' lit up. When he suddenly realised it was lighting he walked straight across without checking if all traffic had stopped. They reached an agreement that when Tim completed the skill correctly ten times in a row they would consider it well and truly acquired. They tested this during the last week of the programme and Tim managed the 'ten in a row' without any difficulty. Kate observed each step carefully and completed the post-test—see page 231. They were both very pleased and celebrated, as planned, in the coffee shop.

Tim's regular and punctual attendance throughout had indicated to Kate that he was very interested in the training programme. She also observed a remarkable change in Tim's communication with her between the first time they had met to discuss the programme and the closing session when they evaluated it and made plans for the future. He had so much more to say for himself and seemed suddenly to be interested in what he was doing and where he was going.

c Generalise the skill

Kate had been careful to build generalisation of the skill into the programme. She had taken steps to ensure that he would be able to use not just the pedestrian crossing adjacent to his work. It had been planned that he would also be familiar with the crossing closest to his home. Due to his quick progress they had time to further generalise the skill, with the result that, by the end of the training programme, Tim was also familiar with the pedestrian crossing near the football club.

The Post-test

CHECKLIST		
Skill: Using a Pedestrian Crossing		
Name: Tim		
	Pre-Test	Post-Test
Can identify the colour red	√	√
Can identify to colour green	0	√
Can associate red with wait	0	√
Can associate green with cross	0	√
Knows what a pedestrian crossing looks like	0	√
Can understand what a pedestrian crossing is for	0	√
Can identify five types of traffic that use the road	(3)	√
Can understand the dangers of careless crossing	0	√
Knows the direction in which to walk	0	√
Can walk safely along the footpath	√	√
Can locate the pedestrian crossing	0	√
Can stand beside the crossing	0	√
Can locate the button to signal wish to cross	0	√
Can locate pedestrian lights opposite	0	√
Knows to press the button	0	√
Can interpret 'standing red man' to mean wait	0	√
Can wait while 'red man' is lighting	0	√
Can concentrate on the signal opposite	0	√
Can observe when the 'green man' lights up	0	√
Can interpret a 'walking green man' to mean cross	0	√
Can check to ensure that all traffic has stopped	0	√
Can walk straight across the road without delay	0	√
Knows the direction in which to walk on the far side	0	√
Test(s) completed	18/4/94	17/6/94

Tim's lifestyle had not yet changed sufficiently to incorporate the newly acquired skill on a daily basis. Kate was aware of this and the potential danger, therefore, was that the skill could fade and be forgotten. She made plans with Tim to ensure that, after all their hard work, this would not happen. She normally bought a newspaper each day on her way home, and she asked Tim if he would mind going to the shop across the road from the workshop for her each day at lunch time. This necessitated him using the pedestrian crossing with which he had become familiar. He was glad of the opportunity to do something for her and could also practise daily use of the crossing. The first couple of times Kate observed how he managed the crossing and then, confident of his ability, she trusted him to manage alone.

d   Make recommendations

Because of the time and effort Kate put in to the initial preparation of the programme, the background work had been completed for all Lifeskills training with Tim for at least the next two years. They both knew exactly what he was aiming for: it was stated clearly in his long-term goal. They had also identified the necessary steps to reach that goal.

Kate's recommendations therefore were simple to identify. The next step in the plan was to learn how to travel by bus, to and from work. She had taken note at the start of the training programme that he required some assertiveness skills and decided that it would be appropriate to include some training sessions on this subject at the start of the next programme.

She found that her involvement in Lifeskills training greatly increased her job satisfaction. She *knew* that she had contributed significantly to improving the quality of Tim's life and this gave her a real sense of achievement.

Select Bibliography

Hobson, B., and Scally, M. (1989). *Lifeskills Teaching*. Maidenhead: McGraw Hill.
(Particularly useful with adults who have mild learning disabilities.)

Priestley, P., McGuire, J., Flegg, D., Hemsley, V., and Welham, D. (1978). *Social Skills and Personal Problem Solving: A handbook of methods*. London: Routledge.

Carr, J., and Collins, S. (1992). *Working Towards Independence: A practical guide to teaching people with learning disabilities*. Jessica Kingsley Publishers Ltd., 116 Pentonville Road, London N1 9JB.
(Useful with adults who have more severe learning disabilities.)

Best, A. B. (1987). *Steps to Independence: A practical guidance on teaching people with mental and sensory handicaps*. Foreword by G. B. Simon. Kidderminster: BIMH Publications.
(Useful with adults who have more severe learning disabilities.)

Blunden, R. (ed.) (1988). *Ties and Connections: An ordinary community life for people with learning difficulties*. King's Fund Centre, 126 Albert Street, London NW1 7NF.
(Useful with adults who have mild learning disabilities.)

Blunden, R., and Allen, D. (1987). *Facing the Challenge: An ordinary life for people with learning difficulties and challenging behaviour*. King's Fund Centre (address as above).

Towel, D. (1988). *An Ordinary Life in Practice: Developing comprehensive community based services for people with learning disabilities*. King's Fund Centre (address as above).

Baker, B. L., Brightman, A. J., and Hinshaw, S. P. *Towards Independent Living*. Steps to Independence Series, a skills training series for children with special needs. Research Press,

2612 North Mattis Avenue, Champaign, Illinois 61820, USA. (Although written for children, the principles and ideas are very useful and can be applied generally.)

Ellis, J., and Barned, T. (1987). *Lifeskills Training Manual*. Community Service Volunteers, 237 Pentonville Road, London N1 9NJ.
(Useful with adults who have very mild learning disabilities.)

Jupp, K. (1994). *Living a Full Life with learning disabilities*. Human Horizons Series. London: Souvenir Press.

From Coping to Confidence. A staff development resource pack for further education teachers of students with moderate learning difficulties. The pack contains seven modules and a video cassette produced by the Department of Education and Science in conjunction with the Further Education Unit, Oxford Publishing Services, Marlborough Road, Oxford.

Learning Support (1989). A staff development resource pack for those working with learners who have special needs. This package for staff contains ten booklets which outline how to devise and deliver training programmes to people with special needs. It is the outcome of a successful collaboration between three national organisations: the Further Education Unit, Skill (National Bureau for Students with Disabilities) and Training Agency. It promotes a common understanding of the needs of learners with special needs. The Further Education Unit, Grove House, 2–6 Orange Street, London WC2H 7WE.

O'Brien, J., and Lyle O'Brien, C. (1989). *Framework for Accomplishment*. Responsive Systems Associates, Atlanta, Georgia, USA.

Power, K. *Focus on the Individual*. Ed. B. McCormack. Open Training College, Dublin City University, Glasnevin, Dublin 9, Ireland.

McCormack, B., and Carroll, D. (eds.) *Survival after the Day Service*. A development of the National Conference on Family Support, held in Dublin in 1989, which looks at issues such as The Parent agenda, family-to-family support and developing a framework for the future. Wordwell Ltd and St Michael's House, PO Box 69, Bray, Co. Wicklow, Ireland.

ALBSU. *Setting up Workplace Basic Skills Training: Guidelines for Practitioners*. A special development project. ALBSU,

Kingsbourne House, 229–231 High Holborn, London WC1V 7DA.

Noonan-Walsh, P. (ed.). *Creating Work Opportunities for Europeans with Mental Handicap*. St Michael's House, Research Department, Upper Kilmacud Road, Stillorgan, Co. Dublin, Ireland.

McConkey, R., and Conliffe, C. (eds.). *The Person with a Mental Handicap: Preparation for an adult life in the community*. St Michael's House, Research Department, Upper Kilmacud Road, Stillorgan, Co. Dublin, Ireland, and Institute of Counselling and Personnel Development, Belfast, N. Ireland.

McConkey, R., and McGinley, P. (eds.) (1992). *Innovations in Employment, Training and Work for People with Learning Difficulties*. Lisieux Hall, Whittle-le-Woods, Chorley, Lancashire PR6 7DX.

McConkey, R., and McGinley, P. (eds.) (1990). *Innovations in Leisure and Recreation for People with a Mental Handicap*. Lisieux Hall (address as above).

Walsh, J. (1986). *Let's Make Friends*. Human Horizons Series. London: Souvenir Press.
(The book outlines and evaluates schemes to develop friendships and links between people who have learning disabilities and their community.)

Mouly, G. J. (1968). *Psychology for Effective Teaching*. Atlanta, Georgia: Holt, Rinehart & Winston.

Forest, M., Snow, J., and O'Brien, J. *Action for Inclusion*. Responsive Systems Associates, Atlanta, Georgia, USA.

Index